Foreword by
Arvind Singh
(Former Tourism Secretary, GOI)

TOURISM AND SOFT POWER DIPLOMACY

Reflections of India's G20 Presidency

Dr. Aishwarya Singh Raikwar

BLUEROSE PUBLISHERS
India | U.K.

Copyright © Dr. Aishwarya Singh Raikwar 2025

All rights reserved by author. No part of this publication may be reproduced, stored in a retrieval system or transmitted in any form or by any means, electronic, mechanical, photocopying, recording or otherwise, without the prior permission of the author. Although every precaution has been taken to verify the accuracy of the information contained herein, the publisher assumes no responsibility for any errors or omissions. No liability is assumed for damages that may result from the use of information contained within.

BlueRose Publishers takes no responsibility for any damages, losses, or liabilities that may arise from the use or misuse of the information, products, or services provided in this publication.

For permissions requests or inquiries regarding this publication, please contact:

BLUEROSE PUBLISHERS
www.BlueRoseONE.com
info@bluerosepublishers.com
+91 8882 898 898
+4407342408967

ISBN: 978-93-7018-767-2

Cover Design: Aman Sharma
Typesetting: Pooja Sharma

First Edition: February 2025

Also by the Same Author

A Quest to Infinity

Dedication

"To my beloved late parents, Smt. Pramila Singh and Thakur Chandra Pratap Singh, and my late grandparents, Smt. Mridula Rani Singh and Satyapal Singh, whose unwavering love, sacrifices, and dreams have shaped the person I am today."

This book is a tribute to your unwavering faith in me, a reflection of the values you instilled, and a humble offering to the legacy you left behind. Though time and fate have taken you beyond my reach, your love remains the foundation of my journey and I carry you in my heart, today and always.

Acknowledgement

Writing this book has been a journey of reflection, gratitude, and purpose, and it would not have been possible without the support, guidance, and inspiration of many incredible individuals.

First and foremost, I express my deepest gratitude to my late parents and my late grandparents, whose love, sacrifices, and values continue to illuminate my path. Their unwavering belief in my dreams has been the foundation of my perseverance and success.

A special thanks to Shri Arvind Singh, Former Secretary, Ministry of Tourism, for his valuable insights and guidance.

I am also deeply grateful to the Ministry of Tourism, Ministry of External Affairs, and the G20 Secretariat, where I had the privilege to contribute and learn. The experiences gained during India's G20 Presidency have profoundly influenced my perspectives on soft power diplomacy and global engagement.

I extend my heartfelt thanks to my family, mentors, colleagues, and peers who have played an instrumental role in shaping my academic and professional journey. Your insights, encouragement, and constructive feedback have enriched my understanding and helped refine the ideas presented in this book. My friends and well-wishers, whose support and belief in me have been a source of strength during this writing process. Your words of encouragement have kept me motivated even in moments of doubt.

I would also like to extend my sincere appreciation to BlueRose Publishers and their dedicated team for shaping this book with care and professionalism. Your support in bringing this work to life has been truly invaluable.

Finally, I extend my sincere appreciation to my readers. This book is for you, and I hope it sparks meaningful conversations, insights, and inspiration for India's evolving global narrative.

With immense gratitude,
Aishwarya

Preface

In the heart of India, where the lush landscapes meet the rusted steel of coal mines, a girl child was born in a remote village in Chhattisgarh. This village, steeped in the struggles of mining life, became the backdrop for a journey fuelled by dreams, education and the relentless pursuit of making a difference. My story is not just a personal narrative; it is a testament to the transformative power of education and the indomitable spirit of aspiration that thrives in even the most challenging circumstances.

Growing up in a conservative family, my early life was shaped by the values and dreams of my mother. Despite the limitations of our environment, she envisioned a future where education could break the social norms and pave the way for opportunities for a girl child. Her dreams were not merely her own; they were a collective aspiration for our family and a beacon of hope for me. Every story she shared about perseverance, the importance of knowledge and the value of public service instilled in me a sense of purpose.

In a setting where coal transport dictated the rhythm of life, the possibilities often felt limited. Yet, my mother was determined to ensure that I had access to the education that could transform our narrative. She believed that the Indian government, through its initiatives such as Jawahar Navodaya Vidyalaya (JNV), a residential school providing world class education to the children of rural background and marginalised communities played a crucial role in creating pathways for students like me when I joined JNV.

In my formative years, I found a guiding star in the words and ideas of our beloved Dr. APJ Abdul Kalam. His vision of a developed India, where every citizen could dream and achieve, resonated deeply with me. I started reading his books at a very young age, captivated by his journey from humble beginnings to becoming the President of India. His belief in the power of dreams and the importance of education inspired me to dream bigger. Dr. Kalam's life was a testament to the idea that with dedication and hard work, anyone could overcome adversity. His emphasis on innovation, youth empowerment and service to the nation mirrored my aspirations. I realized that the journey of impacting lives began with education and a commitment to contributing to the greater good.

With each passing day, my desire to make a difference grew stronger. I envisioned a future where I could leverage my education and experiences to create meaningful change. But the journey was not without its challenges including significant setbacks that tested my resolve. One of the most profound moments came when I lost my parents at the age of 20, while my sister was just 15 years old. This event had a deep impact on me and shaped my understanding of resilience. Each obstacle I faced deepened my conviction in the power of perseverance. I learned that achieving meaningful change requires time and unwavering dedication.

Reflecting on my journey, I am immensely grateful for the foundation laid by my upbringing and education. From a small village in Chhattisgarh to working for India's G20 Presidency, each step has been a building block toward a life dedicated to public service and impact. My mother's dreams combined with Dr. Kalam's teachings has instilled in me a profound sense of responsibility towards my country and society at large. They continue to guide me as I strive to contribute positively to the nation building.

As I move forward, I carry the lessons learned from my early days, recognizing the importance of education, community engagement and service. When I talk about my journey, it is not just about personal achievement; it is about creating pathways for young girls, breaking barriers and fostering a culture of hope and empowerment in the remote villages of our country. In a world filled with challenges, I remain committed to being a catalyst for change, ensuring that the dreams of many who have been my constant are nurtured and realized.

Working with the G20 Cell of the Ministry of Tourism was a transformative journey that allowed me to witness and contribute to India's global leadership during its G20 Presidency. As a proud representative of my nation, I had the privilege of shaping and supporting initiatives that showcased India's rich cultural heritage and tourism potential to the world. From coordinating high-level events to promoting sustainable tourism policies, my role was instrumental in highlighting tourism as a powerful tool for diplomacy, economic growth, and cultural exchange. This experience not only deepened my understanding of global governance and multilateral cooperation but also reaffirmed my belief in India's potential to inspire the world through its stories, landscapes, and traditions. It was an honor to be part of a vision that aligned tourism with sustainability, inclusivity, and peace, reflecting the values of "Vasudhaiva Kutumbakam – the world is one family".

In this incredible country, where diversity and resilience thrive, I believe that every individual has the potential to make a lasting impact. It is this belief that propels me forward, determined to contribute to the Viksit Bharat and a brighter future for all.

Jai Hind.

Foreword

India's G20 Presidency was a transformative diplomatic event wherein the nation's values of "Vasudhaiva Kutumbakam" found resonance. Along with other issues of global significance such as sustainable development, climate action and equitable growth, the subject of Tourism emerged as a significant soft power tool, weaving together cultural diplomacy, economic progress and people to people contacts.

This book offers a ring side view and an insightful narrative of how India used the Tourism track negotiations, during the Presidency, to further international collaboration, cultural understanding and sustainable development. As a result, it is a timely effort that captures India's rich heritage and its contemporary vision for Tourism as an engine for global cooperation and development.

The author's unique perspective, shaped by her experience and research in the Tourism sector, will provide readers an engaging account of India's strategies and achievements during this pivotal period. Through vivid accounts and in depth analysis, the book highlights India's leadership in advocating sustainable tourism and inclusive development. The priorities highlighted during the G20 Presidency, from promoting local communities to laying emphasis on green and digital tourism, presented a new roadmap for the international community.

I am delighted to see this comprehensive account that celebrates India's achievements. It should serve as a valuable resource for scholars, policymakers and practitioners interested in tourism and international relations. Let this effort remind us of the transformative power of Tourism: an activity that transcends borders, fosters mutual understanding, promotes people to people contacts and helps build a more peaceful and inclusive world.

Arvind Singh
(Retd. IAS), Former Secretary, Ministry of Tourism,
Government of India

Contents

A Dream Realized From Enthusiast to Contributor in India's G20 1

India at a Glance 5

The G20 (Group of Twenty) 8

India's G20 Presidency 13

India Tourism 39

G20 Meeting in Srinagar 48

G20 Meeting and Tourism 56

India Tourism and Soft Power Diplomacy 59

India as 'Voice of the Global South' 71

India's G20 Presidency! People's G20 Presidency 80

The Global Impact 85

Geopolitical Ambitions Through G20 Presidency 91

Youth and their Emerging Role in Foreign Policy 97

Rising Geopolitical Stature in Changing Global Order 103

India's Economic Rise and its Influence in the World 109

Viksit Bharat Vision and Role of India's Youth 114

India's G20 Legacy 119

References 131

A Dream Realized
From Enthusiast to Contributor
in India's G20

The day India assumed the presidency of the G20 was unforgettable for me. Sitting in Chennai, far from the bustling corridors of power, I was just another distant enthusiast, watching history unfold with a sense of pride and excitement. The idea that India, my India, would lead the world's most powerful economies and chart a course for global cooperation filled me with hope. I never imagined that within one and a half months, I would be living my dream, working with the G20 Cell of the Ministry of Tourism, contributing to the grand vision that I had celebrated from afar.

A Distant Celebration Turned into Reality

When India took over the G20 Presidency, it was a moment of national triumph and like millions across the country, I felt an intimate connection with the occasion. I had followed every headline, read every article and imagined how India could lead with its unique values of inclusivity, sustainability and unity. The vision of "One Earth, One Family, One Future" resonated deeply within me. It was not just a slogan; it was a call to action—a call I thought I would never get to answer directly.

I celebrated quietly, thinking I would remain an admirer, someone who would support this monumental event from a distance. But fate, as it often does, had other plans. Little did I know that in just over a month, I would not only be celebrating the G20 but contributing to it in ways I had never dreamed possible.

Then, the universe conspired. A chance opportunity, a leap of faith and suddenly, my dream wasn't distant anymore. I received the call to join the G20 Cell of the Ministry of Tourism. I was stunned, speechless even, not fully believing that the same initiative I had admired from a distance had drawn me into its heart. The passion I had harboured in quiet reflection now had an outlet. I was no longer an observer but a participant and the G20 presidency was not just a national achievement; it became personal.

The excitement was overwhelming and the thought of working on something as grand and meaningful as the G20 gave me a rush of ambition and purpose.

I realized that this was not just an opportunity for me; it was a chance to serve the country at a moment when the eyes of the world were on us. This was India's moment on the global stage and here I was, no longer a spectator but a participant, entrusted with a role that would allow me to help shape the image of my country for millions of people across the globe.

The Journey Begins

Joining the G20 Cell felt like stepping into a dream. Every day was a whirlwind of excitement, responsibility and discovery. The sheer scale of the work we were involved in left me in awe. We were tasked with showcasing India's incredible diversity, rich culture and unparalleled tourism potential to the world.

It was not just about promoting tourist destinations; it was about telling a story—India's story. Every project, every initiative, every G20 meeting and every destination playing the host to it reflected the spirit of "Vasudhaiva Kutumbakam" the idea that the whole world is one family. I realized that the work we were doing went beyond just managing events or marketing campaigns; it was about representing the heart and soul of India.

What filled me with the deepest sense of purpose was knowing that my efforts were contributing to something bigger than myself. It was also my first interaction with the Indian bureaucracy and governance. It was a humbling experience to be part of a movement that aimed to promote not just India's tourism but its role as a global leader. We were showing the world that India was not only a country of breathtaking landscapes and rich history but also a country with a vision for a sustainable, inclusive future.

Working with the G20 Cell was more than a job—it was a mission it took a toss on my personal life and health but I was so involved that it barely affected me. It was a chance to show how tourism could be a force for unity, a bridge between cultures and a means of fostering understanding in a world that often feels divided. Every day, I was reminded of the responsibility I carried, but with that responsibility came an immense sense of pride.

As India's G20 Presidency concluded and as I write it, my heart swells with the knowledge that I have been part of something truly historic "New Delhi Leaders' Declaration" is a monumental document in the history of G20. I no longer watched it from a distance—I have lived this journey, contributing to it and in my small way, helping India shine on the global stage.

For me, this is not just about work; it is about realizing a dream that once seemed impossible. It is about ambition, passion and the belief that every small action, every idea, can contribute to a larger cause. As India leads the G20, I am filled with gratitude for the opportunity to serve my country at such a pivotal moment.

The road ahead was long and the work was far from done; sometimes we left the Transport Bhawan late at nights but I woke up each day filled with the same excitement I felt the day I first celebrated India's G20 Presidency from my small room in Chennai. Only now when I write this book, I am not just celebrating—I am part of it, I have worked towards a future where India's vision of global unity, sustainability and progress becomes a reality for all.

India at a Glance

The Mother of Democracy, Unique and Diverse Culture and Rising Economic Power

India, the world's largest democracy, is a nation marked by its rich historical tapestry, diverse cultural heritage and burgeoning economic prowess. As a country that harmonizes ancient traditions with modern advancements, India presents a unique and multifaceted identity. This chapter delves into the essence of India, highlighting its democratic ethos, cultural diversity and growing economic influence on the global stage.

India's democratic roots run deep, tracing back to ancient times. The concept of self-governance and public debate can be found in the ancient republics of the Indian subcontinent, such as the Lichchhavis and the Sangha system of the Buddhists. This historical foundation has evolved into a robust modern democracy, established officially in 1947 with India's independence from British rule.

India's democracy is characterized by its pluralism and inclusivity. The country's constitution, adopted in 1950, is one of the most comprehensive in the world, ensuring fundamental rights and freedom for all its citizens. Regular elections, a free press and an independent judiciary are pillars that uphold the democratic structure. Despite its challenges, such as political corruption and social inequalities, India continues to demonstrate the resilience and dynamism of its democratic framework, enabling it to adapt and thrive in a rapidly changing world.

India's cultural landscape is unparalleled in its diversity. Home to over 1.4 billion people, the country boasts a mosaic of languages, religions and traditions. With 22 officially recognized languages and hundreds of dialects, linguistic diversity is a hallmark of Indian culture. Major religions, including Hinduism, Islam, Christianity, Sikhism, Buddhism and Jainism, coexist harmoniously, contributing to India's rich spiritual heritage.

The cultural diversity of India is vividly expressed through its festivals, cuisines, art and architecture. Festivals such as Diwali, Eid, Christmas and Vaisakhi are celebrated with fervour across the nation reflecting its religious pluralism. Indian cuisines, known for its flavourful spices and regional variations, is a culinary treasure trove. The country's artistic heritage is equally impressive, from the classical dances of Bharatanatyam and Kathak to the vibrant folk traditions of *Bhangra* and *Garba*. Modern architectural marvels such as the Statue of Unity, ancient temples and modern skyscrapers exemplify India's ability to blend tradition with innovation.

In recent decades, India has emerged as a significant economic force. The country's economic liberalization in the early 1990s marked a pivotal shift towards a market-oriented economy, leading to rapid growth and development. Today, India is one of the world's largest economies, with a GDP of over $3 trillion.

Several factors contribute to India's economic ascent. A large and youthful population provides a vast labour pool and consumer market. The information technology (IT) sector, centred in cities like Bangalore and Hyderabad, has positioned India as a global hub for software services and innovation. Additionally, sectors such as pharmaceuticals, manufacturing and renewable energy are driving economic diversification and growth.

India's economic rise is also reflected in its increasing influence in global affairs. As a member of the G20, BRICS and other international organizations, India is crucial in shaping global economic policies. Its strategic partnerships with countries like the United States, Japan and Australia further underscore its growing geopolitical significance.

While India's progress is commendable, the nation faces several challenges that must be addressed to sustain its growth trajectory. Socio-economic disparities, infrastructure deficiencies and environmental concerns are critical issues that require comprehensive solutions. Furthermore, fostering inclusive growth, improving education and healthcare systems and ensuring sustainable development are essential for India's future prosperity.

However, these challenges also present opportunities for innovation and reform. India's commitment to renewable energy, digital transformation and skill development initiatives are promising steps towards addressing these issues. By leveraging its demographic dividend, technological advancements and entrepreneurial spirit, India has the potential to overcome obstacles and achieve sustainable and inclusive growth.

India, with its ancient democratic traditions, vibrant cultural diversity and rising economic power, stands as a beacon of resilience and potential. As the mother of democracy, it continues to uphold the values of pluralism and inclusivity. Its unique cultural heritage enriches the global tapestry, while its economic growth signifies a promising future. Navigating the complexities of development and modernity, India is poised to play a pivotal role in shaping the 21st century, offering lessons and inspiration to the world.

The G20 (Group of Twenty)

Is an international forum for governments and central bank governors from 19 countries and the European Union, representing the world's major economies. It was established in 1999 in response to the global financial crises of the late 1990s, with the aim of bringing together industrialized and developing economies to discuss and promote international financial stability.

Origins and Establishment:

1999: The G20 was created following the 1997 Asian Financial Crisis and other global economic disruptions, where it became apparent that the G7 (an earlier, smaller group of the world's major economies) was not broad enough to effectively address all international economic concerns.

Initially, the G20 began as a meeting of "Finance Ministers and Central Bank Governors" to address global financial challenges.

Expansion into Leaders' Summits; 2008: The global financial crisis prompted a shift in the G20's role. It was elevated to the level of Heads of State or Government. The first G20 Leaders' Summit was held in Washington, D.C., marking a new phase in its evolution, transforming the group from a finance-focused body to a broader forum addressing global economic governance.

Since then, annual Leaders' Summits have become central to G20 discussions, covering a wide range of global issues including trade, climate change, healthcare and development.

Membership: The G20 consists of 19 countries and the European Union (EU) until 2023 New Delhi Summit which included African Union (AU) as a permanent member.

Members: Argentina, Australia, Brazil, Canada, China, France, Germany, India, Indonesia, Italy, Japan, Mexico, Russia, Saudi Arabia, South Africa, South Korea, Turkey, United Kingdom and the United States.

Permanent Guests: Spain has been a permanent invitee and other international organizations such as the International Monetary Fund (IMF), World Bank and the United Nations regularly participate.

Key Milestones:

2009 London Summit: In response to the global financial crisis, leaders agreed on coordinated efforts to inject funds into the global economy, strengthen regulation of financial institutions and reform global financial institutions like the IMF and World Bank.

2010 Seoul Summit: Focused on development, marking the G20's shift towards including emerging economies in the global economic conversation.

2015 Antalya Summit: Addressed the global refugee crisis and terrorism in the wake of ISIS's rise.

2020 Riyadh Summit: Held virtually due to the COVID-19 pandemic, with leaders coordinating on global health, economic recovery and vaccine distribution.

Role of the G20:

The G20 is a "Consensus-driven Forum", decisions are not binding but carry significant global influence due to the economic power of the member states. The group represents 85% of global GDP, 75% of international trade and two-thirds of the world's population, giving it substantial weight in shaping global economic policies. The G20 also plays a role in addressing Climate Change, Inequality, Poverty and Health crises, expanding its scope beyond purely financial and economic issues.

G20 Presidencies:

The presidency of the G20 rotates annually among its members. The country holding the presidency sets the agenda for the year, organizes the leaders' summit and hosts various working groups and ministerial meetings. Recent presidencies include:

2023: India

2024: Brazil

2025: South Africa

The G20 continues to be a key platform for international dialogue, particularly in tackling global crises like financial instability, climate change, pandemics and other challenges requiring international cooperation.

The working groups are thematically formed units within the G20 that are intended to ensure a dedicated focus on specific sectors, such as education, climate change, IT, culture, tourism, agriculture and health. The agenda for the ministerial meetings is shaped by the deliberations of these working groups, which subsequently identify potential areas for collaboration among the G20 members.

Why are G20 Summits Significant?

G20 Summits hold significant importance on the global stage for various reasons. Here's a detailed explanation of why these meetings are crucial:

Global Economic Stability and Coordination: G20 meetings bring together the world's largest economies, enabling coordinated policy responses to global economic challenges. This helps in mitigating financial crises and ensuring global economic stability. The G20 played a crucial role during the 2008 financial crisis by coordinating stimulus measures, which helped stabilize the global economy. It continues to be a platform for addressing global financial uncertainties.

Inclusive Global Governance: The G20 includes both developed and emerging economies, representing around 85% of global GDP, 75% of international trade and two-thirds of the world's population. This diverse representation ensures more inclusive global governance. By including major economies from all continents, the G20 fosters international collaboration and consensus-building on key global issues.

Sustainable Development: G20 agendas often focus on sustainable development goals (SDGs), climate change and environmental protection. The group's commitment to these issues drives global efforts and funding towards sustainable practices. In light of the COVID-19 pandemic, G20 meetings have become pivotal in coordinating global health responses, vaccine distribution and preparedness for future pandemics.

Trade and Investment: G20 discussions on trade policies aim to reduce trade barriers and promote fair trade practices which are essential for global economic growth. The meetings encourage investment in infrastructure, technology and innovation which are critical for economic development in member countries.

Financial Regulation and Reform: The G20 works on strengthening global financial regulation to prevent future financial crises. This includes reforms in banking, taxation and financial market regulations. Initiatives like the Base Erosion and Profit Shifting (BEPS) framework aims to combat tax evasion and ensure that multinational companies pay their fair share of taxes.

Political and Diplomatic Significance: G20 summits provide a platform for bilateral and multilateral diplomatic engagements, allowing leaders to discuss and resolve geopolitical issues on the sidelines of the main meetings. These meetings help in building consensus on contentious issues, promoting peace and stability through dialogue and cooperation.

Innovation and Technology: G20 forums discuss the impact of technological advancements and the digital economy, promoting policies that support innovation and address challenges like cybersecurity and digital inequality. Encouraging collaboration in research and development, the G20 helps drive global technological progress and economic growth.

G20 meetings are significant because they serve as a premier forum for international economic cooperation. They address a wide range of global issues, from economic stability and sustainable development to financial regulation and health crisis. The diverse representation and collaborative nature of the G20 make it a crucial platform for fostering global peace, stability and prosperity.

India's G20 Presidency

India's G20 Presidency, spanning from December 2022 to November 2023, marks a pivotal moment in the country's international diplomacy and economic engagement. As the world's largest democracy and one of the fastest-growing major economies, India's leadership in the G20 provided a unique opportunity to shape global economic policies and address pressing international issues. The G20, representing 85% of global GDP, 75% of international trade and two-thirds of the world population, is a vital forum for global economic cooperation. India's presidency focused on fostering inclusive and sustainable development, leveraging digital transformation, enhancing climate action and promoting multilateralism.

Economic Growth and Development

India's G20 Presidency came at a critical time for global economic recovery post-COVID-19. India aimed to advocate for coordinated fiscal policies to stimulate growth and stability. This involved addressing supply chain disruptions, promoting global trade and encouraging investments in key sectors such as infrastructure and healthcare.

Infrastructure and Investment

A significant part of India's agenda is to push for increased investment in infrastructure, which is crucial for long-term economic growth. This includes advocating for enhanced public-private partnerships and innovative financing mechanisms to mobilize resources for large-scale infrastructure projects, especially in developing countries.

Addressing Inequality

India emphasized inclusive growth, focusing on reducing inequalities both within and among countries. This involves promoting policies that ensure equitable access to resources, education, healthcare and economic opportunities. India advocated for international support for social protection programs and poverty alleviation initiatives.

Digital Transformation and Innovation

India showcased its success in developing digital public infrastructure, such as the Aadhaar system and Unified Payments Interface (UPI), which have revolutionized service delivery and financial inclusion. India aims to share best practices and promote the adoption of similar systems in other G20 countries.

India's presidency focused on addressing the digital divide by promoting policies that enhance digital literacy, expand internet connectivity and ensure affordable access to digital technologies. This includes advocating for international cooperation to support the development of digital infrastructure in low-income countries.

India aimed to foster innovation by promoting policies that support startups, research and development and technology transfer. This includes encouraging collaboration between academia, industry and governments to create conducive environments for innovation and entrepreneurship.

Climate Action and Sustainability

India's G20 Presidency highlighted the need for enhanced climate finance to support developing countries in their transition to low-carbon economies. India advocates for developed countries to fulfil their commitments to provide financial assistance and technology transfer to support climate mitigation and adaptation efforts.

India is committed to accelerating the global transition to renewable energy. The presidency emphasizes the importance of investing in clean energy technologies, such as solar and wind power and promoting energy efficiency measures. India also aims to foster international cooperation in developing and deploying innovative energy solutions. Promoting sustainable agricultural practices is a key focus area, with India advocating for policies that support resilient food systems and sustainable land use. This includes encouraging research and development in sustainable farming techniques, promoting agroforestry and enhancing water management practices.

Multilateralism and Global Governance

India's presidency reaffirmed its commitment to strengthening multilateral institutions and promoting a rules-based international order. This involves advocating for reforms to global institutions, such as the United Nations and the World Trade Organization, to make them more inclusive and representative of contemporary realities.

We emphasized the importance of global cooperation in addressing complex international challenges, such as climate change, terrorism and pandemics. The presidency aims to foster dialogue and collaboration among G20 members and other international stakeholders to develop coordinated responses to these challenges.

Health and Pandemic Preparedness

India's G20 Presidency focuses on strengthening global health systems to enhance their resilience against future pandemics.

This includes advocating for increased investment in healthcare infrastructure, workforce training and research and development for new medical technologies. India emphasizes the importance of ensuring equitable access to vaccines and healthcare for all. The presidency advocates for international cooperation to support the development, production and distribution of vaccines, especially in low and middle-income countries.

India aims to strengthen global mechanisms for early detection, rapid response and effective management of health emergencies. This includes promoting international collaboration on pandemic preparedness and response, as well as enhancing the role of the World Health Organization in coordinating global health efforts.

Social Inclusion and Gender Equality

Promoting gender equality and empowering women is a central theme of India's G20 Presidency. India advocates for policies that support women's economic participation, leadership and access to education and healthcare. This includes promoting women's entrepreneurship and addressing barriers to women's participation in the workforce.

There is a need to address social disparities and promote inclusive development. This involves advocating for policies that support marginalized communities, including those based on caste, ethnicity and socioeconomic status. India aims to promote social protection programs and initiatives that enhance social mobility and inclusion.

India's G20 Presidency represented a significant opportunity for the country to influence global policy and address some of the most pressing challenges of our time. Through its focus on economic growth, digital transformation, climate action, multilateralism, health and social inclusion, India aims to foster a more inclusive, sustainable and resilient world. The presidency has not only enhanced India's global standing but also reinforces its role as a key player in shaping the future of international cooperation and development.

India's G20 Presidency has achieved significant milestones in promoting global economic stability, digital transformation, climate action, multilateralism, health and social inclusion. These achievements reflect India's commitment to fostering a more inclusive, sustainable and resilient world. The presidency has not only enhanced India's global standing but also reinforced its role as a key player in shaping the future of international cooperation and development. Through its leadership, India has demonstrated the power of collaboration and the importance of addressing global challenges collectively.

India's rich legacy in G20 will not only be known for the inclusion of Arican Union but also for the India-Middle East-Europe Corridor (IMEC). The recent G20 meeting in New Delhi inaugurated a $20 billion IMEC which is an ambitious multi-faceted network designed to facilitate the sustainable and efficient movement of products and services between Europe and Asia through the Middle East. The G20 nations participating in this initiative will convene subsequent meetings to formulate an action plan with specified timelines for execution.

India's G20 Presidency is widely recognized for producing the highest number of outcome documents compared to previous presidencies, with a significant number of adopted declarations, reports and policy priorities across various working groups solidifying its reputation for a highly productive and impactful leadership on the global stage.

About India's G20 presidency and outcome documents:

High volume of documents:

During its presidency, India generated a significantly higher number of outcome documents compared to previous G20 chairs, including detailed reports, policy proposals and consensus declarations across various sectors like climate action, digital public infrastructure and development financing.

Focus on Global South concerns:

India actively championed the interests of developing countries, incorporating their priorities into the outcome documents, highlighting issues like debt relief and climate finance.

"New Delhi Leaders' Declaration":

The final summit concluded with the adoption of the "New Delhi Leaders' Declaration", considered a key achievement encapsulating the consensus reached on various critical issues.

Impact on multilateralism:

By delivering a large volume of comprehensive outcome documents, India is seen as having revitalized multilateralism and strengthened the G20 platform.

The G20, as a premier forum for international economic cooperation, operates through multiple working groups and engagement groups to address global challenges. The G20 process is divided into two major tracks: The Finance Track and the Sherpa Track. India also held meetings and discussions with various engagement groups comprising non-government participants from each G20 member to provide recommendations to the G20 Leaders and contribute towards the policy-making process such as Youth20, Think20, Women20, Science20, Parliament20, Urban20, Civil20, SAI20, Startup20, Labour20 and Business20.

1. Finance Track:

The Finance Track deals with economic, financial and monetary issues primarily led by finance ministers and central bank governors. Key topics include:

- Global economic growth
- Sustainable finance
- Taxation
- Financial regulation
- International financial architecture

2. Sherpa Track:

The Sherpa Track addresses non-financial global issues such as development, climate change, trade, energy, health, agriculture and more. Sherpas are representatives from each member country who coordinate this track. It includes various working groups, such as:

- Development Working Group (DWG): Focused on sustainable development, Sustainable Development Goals, and socio-economic issues.
- Climate Sustainability Working Group: Tackles climate action, environmental sustainability and green transitions.
- Tourism Working Group (TWG): Focused on tourism development, recovery post-pandemic, sustainable tourism and cultural heritage.
- Trade and Investment Working Group: Deals with issues of international trade, global value chains and investments.

Tourism Working Group (TWG):

During India's G20 Presidency, the Tourism Working Group played a crucial role; especially considering the country's vast and diverse tourism sector. The TWG underlined the importance of tourism in economic recovery, sustainability and cultural preservation. The group focused on creating frameworks that could aid the global tourism sector post-pandemic, leveraging India's unique cultural heritage, natural landscapes and tourism potential.

India's G20 Tourism Working Group meetings played a pivotal role in shaping a more resilient, sustainable, and inclusive global tourism sector with a particular focus on rural communities, digital innovations, and cultural preservation. The insights and frameworks developed through these meetings are essential for revitalizing tourism globally, ensuring it contributes positively to local economies and environmental sustainability.

1st TWG (7th February - 9th February, 2023)

Source: Ministry of Tourism, Govt. of India

The first Tourism Working Group meeting under India's G20 Presidency, set against the stunning landscape of the Rann of Kutch, was a vivid illustration of the country's cultural splendour and natural beauty. This vast salt desert, stretching like an endless sea of white, created a surreal backdrop as delegates from across the globe arrived for the gathering.

As the sun began to rise, casting its golden hue over the pristine white expanse, a row of vibrant tents and traditional *Bhungas* (round, mud-walled huts) stood out like jewels. Adorned with intricate mirror work, the venue reflected the traditional craftsmanship of the Kutch region, symbolizing India's deep-rooted heritage and the harmonious blend of progress and preservation.

Delegates were welcomed with the beats of *Dhols* and folk dancers swirling in colourful attire, their movements mirroring the rhythms of the desert wind. The spirit of **"Atithi Devo Bhava"** (Guest is God) was palpable in every gesture, as the local community embraced visitors with warmth and hospitality.

The discussions began in a large, beautifully decorated marquee. Inside, against the backdrop of large screens displaying the breath-taking landscapes of India's diverse tourist destinations, speakers engaged in conversations about sustainable tourism, leveraging digitalization and empowering local communities. These discussions resonated with the broader *theme of India's G20 Presidency: "One Earth, One Family, One Future."*

As the meetings unfolded, the delegates ventured outside for a unique experience—sunset at the Great Rann. The white salt plains turned shades of pink and orange as the sun dipped below the horizon, leaving everyone in awe of nature's artistry. The calmness of the moment was only interrupted by the gentle music of the local Kutchi instruments, serenading the guests as they stood in silence, reflecting on the unspoken beauty of this place.

Source: Ministry of Tourism, Govt. of India

Evenings were a celebration of India's cultural mosaic. A grand cultural performance was organized showcasing the vibrant traditions of Gujarat. Dressed in their elaborate costumes, Kathakali dancers shared the stage with local Kutchi folk performances while a fusion of classical Indian and modern global music filled the air. Delegates savoured authentic Kutchi cuisine served in an open-air setting under a starry sky, making the evening even more magical.

Throughout the meeting, the symbolism of the Rann of Kutch, a place where the land meets the sea in a vast-harmonious union, resonated with the theme of global unity in addressing challenges. The discussions on sustainable tourism, rural development and community engagement carried extra weight in this serene yet harsh environment—reminding everyone that preserving the delicate balance between nature and development is critical.

In the end, the Rann of Kutch not only served as the physical venue for the first Tourism Working Group meeting but also as a metaphor—a place where nations gathered to bridge divides, celebrate cultural diversity and craft a future of inclusive, sustainable tourism for the world.

2nd TWG (2nd Apr - 4th Apr, 2023)

Source: Ministry of Tourism, Govt. of India

The second Tourism Working Group meeting of India's G20 Presidency unfolded amidst the mist-laden hills of Siliguri and Darjeeling, where the majestic Eastern Himalayas served as a breath-taking backdrop. This gathering took place in a setting that combined the tranquil beauty of the mountains with the vibrant charm of India's tea country, symbolizing the convergence of nature, culture and innovation.

As the delegates arrived, a cool breeze carrying the fresh scent of tea leaves welcomed them to the highlands. Siliguri, often known as the "Gateway to the Northeast," served as the starting point of their journey. But it was Darjeeling, with its rolling tea estates and panoramic views of the Kanchenjunga—the third-highest mountain in the world—that truly captured the essence of the meeting. The snowy peaks seemed to watch over the gathering as the delegates set their sights on shaping the future of tourism.

A historic toy train, the iconic Darjeeling Himalayan Railway, transported the group to their destination. Its rhythmic chugging up the steep, winding tracks echoed the theme of sustainable and inclusive tourism that framed the discussions ahead. The train ride itself, a UNESCO World Heritage experience, was a reminder of how tourism can intertwine history, culture and nature, creating lasting memories while preserving local identity.

The venue, a colonial-era estate nestled amidst the tea gardens, had been transformed into a hub of international dialogue. The meeting rooms overlooked emerald slopes dotted with tea pluckers, their brightly coloured clothing creating splashes of vibrant hues in the lush green fields. This scenic setting grounded the discussions in one of the meeting's central topics: eco-tourism and how it can empower local communities while preserving the environment.

Inside, against the backdrop of large windows framing the towering mountains, global leaders engaged in conversations on digital transformation in tourism, the revitalization of small businesses and community-led initiatives. The serene ambiance of the hills seemed to inspire collaboration, fostering an atmosphere where different voices and perspectives merged into a collective vision.

During the meeting breaks, delegates were treated to a series of immersive experiences showcasing the region's cultural and natural wealth. They visited tea estates, where they observed the intricate process of tea cultivation and plucking. A tea-tasting session was arranged, offering a glimpse into the rich Flavors of Darjeeling's world-renowned teas, with local experts explaining the delicate art of tea blending. Each cup of tea served was a celebration of the centuries of tradition of the people of the land.

The evenings were equally enchanting, with cultural performances illuminating the vibrant diversity of the region. Sherpa dancers in traditional attire showcased their rhythmic steps while Lepcha musicians filled the air with soulful tunes from bamboo flutes. The essence of North Bengal's tribal and ethnic culture blended harmoniously with the international gathering, underscoring the theme of cultural exchange as a cornerstone of global tourism.

The culmination of the meeting was a sunrise viewing from Tiger Hill, Darjeeling's most famous vantage point. As delegates huddled under blankets, sipping hot masala chai, the first rays of the sun kissed the peaks of Kanchenjunga, turning them from pale pink to golden orange. In that moment, as the Himalayas glowed in the morning light, the global conversation on sustainable tourism seemed to find its perfect metaphor: just as the sun gradually illuminates the mountain, so too could collaborative global efforts bring about a brighter, more sustainable future for tourism.

The second Tourism Working Group meeting in Siliguri and Darjeeling had been more than just a meeting of minds—it was an experience that merged nature, culture and global policy in one of the most stunning landscapes on Earth. As the delegates departed, they carried with them not only the outcomes of their discussions but also the serene spirit of the Himalayas, a reminder of the delicate balance between development and preservation that defines the future of tourism.

Story time;

The meeting happened in Darjeeling & Siliguri, West Bengal. The delegation and officials stayed in Siliguri and travelled to Darjeeling for meetings and excursions. On the last day, we were taken to the historic Ghum station for the Toy Train ride of the Darjeeling Himalayan Railway, a UNESCO World Heritage site. As the region falls in hilly terrain, residents' lives were disrupted due to the G20 event. On the day of the visit, the roads were blocked for public due to protocol reasons. In these circumstances, we generally assume that the people could be a little annoyed due to the disruption of their daily peaceful schedule. Still, the generosity of the people there filled my heart with pride. People stood on both sides of the roads waving hands and flags, smiling and welcoming the delegates when the convoy reached Ghum station. The streets were flooded with smiling locals. The shopkeepers, the children, the old and the young, everyone present there were smiling. A sight I will carry with me for a lifetime! A gesture that is not usual, but welcome to the stories of Incredible India and its Incredible People!

Diplomatic Engagements to Encourage Participation in the G20 Meeting in Kashmir

India's presidency of the G20 in 2023 marked a significant milestone in its diplomatic history. The country's strategic decision to host a G20 meeting in Kashmir was a bold move aimed at showcasing the region's potential for peace, development and international cooperation. A key part of this effort involved engaging with ambassadors and foreign ministers stationed in New Delhi to ensure their participation in this highly symbolic event.

This chapter delves into the diplomatic process behind the scenes, highlighting the meetings held with ambassadors and foreign ministers, the challenges faced and the strategies employed to encourage their participation in the G20 meeting in Kashmir.

Preparing for Diplomatic Engagement

Prior to engaging foreign dignitaries, the Indian government conducted thorough preparations to ensure that the right message was conveyed during these crucial meetings. The Ministry of External Affairs, in collaboration with the G20 Cell of the Ministry of Tourism, designed a roadmap for outreach.

Key components of this preparation included:

Comprehensive Briefings: Indian diplomats, along with key officials from the Ministry of Tourism and other governmental bodies, prepared comprehensive presentations highlighting Kashmir's natural beauty, investment potential and security improvements in the region.

Strategic Messaging: Emphasis was placed on promoting Kashmir as a hub for sustainable tourism, international cooperation and cultural exchange. This aligned with G20's focus on inclusive development, making it a compelling argument for holding a meeting in the region.

Risk Management and Security Protocols: Given the geopolitical sensitivity of Kashmir, a robust plan addressing potential security concerns was put in place. The Indian government showcased its readiness to provide full security for all delegates, assuring them of a safe environment.

Diplomatic Engagements: The Process

Initial Outreach to Foreign Embassies

The first step involved reaching out to the diplomatic missions in New Delhi. The Ministry of External Affairs and Ministry of Tourism sent formal invitations to ambassadors and foreign ministers, inviting them to a series of meetings to discuss the G20 agenda and the proposed Kashmir event. These invitations underscored the historical significance of Kashmir and the Indian government's commitment to promoting peace and development in the region.

Meeting Ambassadors: Bilateral Conversations Face-to-face meetings with ambassadors were a critical component of the outreach. These one-on-one conversations provided Indian diplomats with an opportunity to address individual concerns and highlight the strategic importance of the G20 meeting in Kashmir. Discussions revolved around:

The Role of G20 in Promoting Regional Stability: India positioned the Kashmir event as an opportunity for global powers to engage in a region traditionally seen as politically sensitive.

Economic Opportunities: The Indian side emphasized the region's potential for tourism, trade and investment, aligning these opportunities with the broader goals of the G20.

Security Assurances: Security was a significant concern, especially for nations that had traditionally been cautious about their engagements in Kashmir. India provided detailed plans outlining the security measures in place, working to build trust with sceptical ambassadors.

Engaging Foreign Ministers: High-Level Diplomacy At a higher level, meetings with foreign ministers required even more strategic diplomacy. Here, India focused on building bilateral relations while making the case for the G20 event. These discussions often extended beyond Kashmir, touching on larger geopolitical dynamics and India's role in the international community. Topics included:

India's G20 Presidency: Foreign ministers were briefed on India's G20 agenda, which emphasized inclusive development, climate action and sustainable tourism—issues that aligned with the proposed event in Kashmir.

Regional Geopolitics: India's decision to hold a G20 meeting in Kashmir was inherently geopolitical. These discussions allowed Indian officials to position the event as a message of peace and stability in South Asia, appealing to foreign ministers' broader foreign policy objectives.

Challenges and Diplomatic Hurdles

Despite India's best efforts, securing unanimous support from all G20 nations was not without its challenges. A few countries expressed hesitance, citing historical tensions between India and Pakistan, while others were cautious about the optics of hosting such a high-profile event in a disputed territory. Some Western countries, particularly those with significant Pakistani communities or ties to Pakistan, were wary of the potential backlash at home.

India, however, handled these challenges with diplomatic finesse. Special envoys were sent to nations expressing hesitance and customized security guarantees were given to alleviate concerns. Additionally, India leveraged its growing clout on the global stage as an emerging economic and political power to garner support from undecided countries.

Positive Outcomes and Success Stories

Despite the diplomatic complexities, India's engagement with ambassadors and foreign ministers resulted in a largely positive response. The G20 meeting in Kashmir saw participation from a wide range of countries, many of whom publicly praised India for its handling of the event. The meeting not only highlighted Kashmir's potential for development but also strengthened India's role as a leader in global diplomacy.

After visiting Kashmir, some ambassadors shared positive feedback about the region's natural beauty and cultural richness. This marked a significant step in changing the global narrative around Kashmir showing that it could host high-profile international events in a peaceful and secure manner.

The diplomatic engagement with ambassadors and foreign ministers was a crucial aspect of India's G20 presidency, especially in the context of organizing a meeting in Kashmir. Through careful planning, transparent communication and strategic negotiations, India managed to overcome many of the challenges associated with the decision. The event not only placed Kashmir in the global spotlight but also demonstrated India's growing influence in international diplomacy. This chapter exemplifies how targeted diplomatic outreach can shape perceptions and foster international collaboration, even in politically sensitive regions.

3rd TWG (22nd May – 24th May, 2023)

The third Tourism Working Group meeting under India's G20 Presidency unfolded in the serene valley of Srinagar, Kashmir—a land often described as "paradise on earth." Nestled between snow-capped mountains and surrounded by pristine lakes and lush gardens, this meeting felt like a dreamscape brought to life. Srinagar's natural beauty, combined with its rich cultural heritage, provided the perfect setting to discuss the future of sustainable tourism and global unity.

As the G20 delegates arrived, they were greeted by a crisp mountain breeze and the sight of *shikaras* (traditional wooden boats) gliding over the tranquil waters of Dal Lake. The lake, reflecting the snow-capped peaks of the Zabarwan Range, sparkled under the soft light of the afternoon sun. The *shikaras*, adorned with vibrant Kashmiri carpets and cushions, ferried the delegates to the iconic houseboats where they would be staying. This experience encapsulated the seamless blend of heritage and hospitality that Kashmir is renowned for.

Source: Ministry of Tourism, Govt. of India

4th TWG and Tourism Ministerial Meeting (19th June – 22nd June, 2023)

The fourth and final Tourism Working Group meeting of India's G20 Presidency unfolded against the sun-drenched shores of Goa, where the Arabian Sea meets lush palm-fringed beaches. Goa, known for its vibrant culture, historic charm and laid-back vibe, provided the perfect setting for this conclusive gathering—a place where delegates could reflect on the journey so far, while diving into the future of tourism with renewed energy.

The grand finale of India's G20 Tourism Working Group journey culminated in the Tourism Ministers Meeting in Goa, where the energy of months of dialogue and collaboration crystallized into a vision for the future of global tourism. Set against the picturesque backdrop of Goa's sun-kissed beaches and tropical allure, this meeting brought together the most influential voices in tourism—ministers, global leaders and industry experts from across the world—ready to chart a new course for tourism in the post-pandemic world.

Source: Ministry of Tourism, Govt. of India

The venue for the meeting was stunning Taj Hotel, where the azure waters of the Arabian Sea stretched endlessly into the horizon, symbolizing the infinite potential of the discussions ahead. Palm trees swayed gently in the breeze, casting dappled shadows over the white pavilions where the delegates would gather. This fusion of nature's tranquillity and purposeful dialogue set the tone for an atmosphere of collaboration and forward-thinking.

As the ministers and dignitaries arrived, they were greeted with a traditional Goan welcome—flower garlands, soulful Konkani music and the sweet fragrance of marigolds. The setting itself embodied Goa's duality—modern luxury mingled with the echoes of its Portuguese past, from the colonial-style architecture of the venue to the tiled courtyards shaded by centuries-old banyan trees. The air buzzed with anticipation, reflecting the importance of this moment, not just for India, but for the global tourism industry that had faced immense challenges in recent years.

The fourth Tourism Working Group meeting in Goa was not just the culmination of months of dialogue—it was a celebration of tourism's power to transcend borders, build connections and preserve the world's most precious resources. Goa, with its blend of history, nature and festivity, had offered the perfect conclusion to a journey that promised a brighter, more sustainable future for global tourism.

On the side-lines, ministers also engaged in bilateral meetings, where partnerships were forged, agreements signed and commitments made to drive cross-border tourism cooperation. There was a palpable sense of global unity, a shared understanding that tourism's challenges—climate change, overtourism, economic disparity—could only be tackled through collective action.

A highlight of the meeting was a special Heritage Walk through the heart of Old Goa and Lower Aguada Jail Museum where the delegates explored the historic churches, cathedrals and convents that stand as a testament to Goa's unique blend of Indian and Portuguese influences. As they strolled through these centuries-old monuments, discussions naturally shifted toward the protection of cultural heritage sites and the importance of involving local communities in their preservation.

As the delegates departed Goa, there was a sense of achievement and optimism. The meeting had not only set new benchmarks for tourism policy but had also fostered a deeper understanding of tourism's ability to heal, connect and uplift. Goa, with its scenic beauty and rich cultural tapestry, had provided the perfect stage for this transformative moment and the closing of India's G20 Tourism Working Group meetings left a legacy that would inspire the global tourism community for years to come.

The vision of sustainable, inclusive and resilient tourism was now firmly in the hands of the world's leaders, ready to be realized, with Goa's shimmering shores serving as a reminder of what is at stake—and what can be achieved—when the world works together.

New Delhi Leaders' Summit (September 9–10, 2023)

The grand crescendo of India's G20 Presidency was the New Delhi Leaders' Summit, a gathering that united the world's most influential leaders in the heart of India's capital. Against the iconic backdrop of New Delhi's historic architecture and its thriving modernity, this summit embodied the vision of global collaboration, where the challenges of today would be met with bold, collective action to shape a prosperous and sustainable future.

The summit was hosted at the sprawling Pragati Maidan International Convention Centre, Bharat Mandapam, a state-of-the-art venue that symbolized India's forward-looking spirit. The grand building, with its sweeping lines and intricate designs inspired by traditional Indian motifs, stood as a blend of the old and the new, mirroring the ethos of the summit itself—honouring the past while crafting a future of innovation and cooperation.

New Delhi, with its rich cultural and political history, provided a profound sense of occasion for the leaders' gathering. As the motorcades arrived along tree-lined avenues, flanked by the red sandstone domes of Lutyens' Delhi, the leaders were welcomed with a ceremonial display of India's rich heritage. An ensemble of musicians played traditional Indian instruments like the *sitar* and *tabla*, while flower petals showered down from above, representing peace and unity.

The opening ceremony took place in the expansive central hall, where the Prime Minister of India delivered a stirring address, underscoring the *G20's theme: "Vasudhaiva Kutumbakam"—One Earth, One Family, One Future.* His words resonated deeply with the assembled leaders, emphasizing the need for multilateralism and global solidarity in addressing the most pressing challenges of our time—climate change, global health, economic inequality and digital transformation. The screens behind him displayed visuals of India's landscapes, from the Himalayas to the Ganges, reinforcing the summit's focus on sustainability and the need to preserve the planet's fragile ecosystems.

The discussions in New Delhi were built around key priorities of India's G20 Presidency: green development, digital transformation, inclusive growth and equitable healthcare. In the breakout sessions, world leaders and their delegations engaged in intense dialogues about reshaping the global economic order, addressing the climate crisis and reducing inequality between nations. There was a palpable sense of urgency in the air and the leaders were determined to translate words into concrete action.

Amidst these critical discussions, the leaders were treated to a series of cultural and artistic experiences that brought to life the vibrancy of India's heritage. One evening, the *Rashtrapati Bhavan* (Presidential Palace) hosted a cultural gala, where leaders walked through the magnificent Mughal Gardens before being seated under a canopy of stars for a grand performance. Classical Indian dancers performed intricate Bharatanatyam and Kathak routines, their movements narrating ancient tales of love and valour, while musicians played haunting melodies on the sarod and flute, creating an atmosphere of timeless elegance. The gala was a celebration of India's soft power, demonstrating how culture and diplomacy intertwine to build bridges across nations.

The final day of the summit was marked by a symbolic planting of trees at *Raj Ghat*, Mahatma Gandhi's memorial, where the leaders gathered in quiet reflection. The trees, representing each member nation of the G20, were planted to symbolize unity and growth, a commitment to a greener, more sustainable future.

Standing together in this solemn space, the leaders paid homage to Gandhi's ideals of peace, non-violence and global harmony.

As the summit ended, the leaders convened for the final Declaration of New Delhi, a historic document that laid out the path forward for addressing global challenges. The declaration emphasized climate action, inclusive economic recovery, global health equity and the responsible use of technology. It was a declaration of intent, a call for cooperation in a world increasingly divided and a pledge to work together for the common good.

In the final moments of the summit, the Prime Minister of India, flanked by the leaders of the world's most powerful nations, took centre stage for the handing over of the G20 Presidency. As the ceremonial baton passed to the next host country Brazil, there was a sense of accomplishment—a recognition that, while many challenges remained, the G20 had reaffirmed its role as a beacon of hope for collective global action.

New Delhi's grand summit had not only showcased the city's historical grandeur and cultural diversity but had also cemented the G20's role as a vital platform for shaping a more equitable, sustainable and connected world. The legacy of the summit would ripple far beyond the halls of Bharat Mandapam, inspiring future generations to carry forward the spirit of global cooperation.

India Tourism

India's tourism industry holds significant potential on the global stage. India is a country with immense cultural diversity, historical significance, natural beauty and a wide range of attractions, which make it a popular destination for tourists from around the world. The country boasts a rich cultural heritage with numerous UNESCO World Heritage Sites, its historical landmarks and vibrant festivals attract history enthusiasts and cultural travellers. The Indian government has been taking steps to promote tourism through campaigns like "Incredible India" and by easing visa regulations to attract more tourists.

India's G20 presidency has given a boost to the tourism and hospitality sector. The G20 meetings held in different corners of the country have placed these Indian cities on the global tourism map. The visits by international delegates have resulted in improved infrastructure, including airports, highways and hotels; it has enhanced accessibility and comfort for locals as well.

The country's diverse geography offers opportunities for various types of tourism such as beach tourism (Peninsular India), mountain tourism (Himalayas), desert tourism (Rajasthan) and wildlife tourism (national parks and sanctuaries). India is the birthplace of various religions and spiritual practices. Places like Varanasi, Bodh Gaya and Rishikesh attract spiritual seekers. Additionally, the country offers yoga and wellness retreats that have gained popularity internationally. The diverse landscape of India provides opportunities for adventure activities such as trekking, mountaineering, river rafting and more. The Himalayan region and regions like Himachal Pradesh and Uttarakhand are popular for adventure tourism.

India has become a hub for medical tourism due to its advanced medical facilities and cost-effective healthcare services. Patients from around the world travel to India for medical treatments and surgeries. The government has recently introduced the AYUSH visa aiming at the ease of travelling for foreigners seeking medical services in India. Wellness tourism is also getting attention post-COVID-19 and India has some renowned wellness destinations in states like Kerala, Uttarakhand, Maharashtra and Karnataka. The country's Indian cuisine is renowned globally for its flavours and variety. Food enthusiasts are drawn to explore the diverse culinary traditions across different regions of the country.

India has successfully conducted over 200 meetings of the G20 in more than 60 destinations. The Indian government recognizing the potential of MICE tourism has taken steps to promote and facilitate this sector. This includes initiatives to ease visa procedures for business travellers and support for the development of MICE infrastructure. India is home to a growing number of industries, IT hubs and multinational corporations. These business clusters attract both domestic and international business travellers making it an ideal location for hosting meetings and conferences.

Many cities in India have developed world-class convention centres, exhibition halls and conference facilities that can accommodate large gatherings. Cities like Delhi, Mumbai, Bangalore, Hyderabad and Chennai offer modern infrastructure for hosting various MICE events.

India's major cities are well-connected with international flights, enhancing accessibility for international participants attending MICE events. From luxury hotels to boutique accommodations, India offers a wide range of lodging options that cater to different budgets and preferences. India's wellness and medical tourism industry also add value to MICE tourism. Participants can combine their business events with health and wellness activities, such as yoga retreats or Ayurvedic treatments. Combining business with leisure is a trend in MICE tourism. India's rich cultural heritage, historical sites and tourist attractions offer participants the opportunity to explore the country's unique culture and history during their visit.

It was long considered notion while major cities have modern facilities, some smaller cities might lack adequate infrastructure for hosting large-scale events. But the way India's tier-II and tier-III cities have performed during G20 is remarkable. Yes, India faces competition from other countries that have well-established tourism sectors. Despite the vast potential, India's tourism industry has faced challenges such as concerns about safety and security, sanitation and hygiene, infrastructure gaps in some areas and regulatory hurdles. The authorities are striving to reduce that gap to harness the full potential of this sector.

India's digital transformation journey is remarkable and is being used as a case study by many. The pandemic accelerated the adoption of digital technologies in the tourism industry as well. Online bookings, virtual tours, contactless experiences and digital health verifications became essential tools for the new normal. Sustainable tourism practices were gaining prominence before the pandemic and continued to be important. Travelers, governments and organizations are increasingly focused on environmentally friendly and socially responsible travel. The advancements of Sustainable Development Goals have been at the forefront of India's agenda for the discussions in G20 meetings.

The COVID-19 pandemic had a profound impact on global tourism. Building resilience in tourism, diversification of tourism offerings, investment in local infrastructure and crisis management planning have gained importance in recent times. Tourists showing increased interest in less crowded destinations, rural areas and outdoor activities and the trend towards experiential travel and authentic cultural experiences brings a unique opportunity for India Tourism.

India as a Rising MICE Destination

India has some world class events hosting capabilities and it hosted a series of G20 meetings across various cities in 2023 as part of its G20 presidency. The metros are quite popular for having excellent MICE facilities but India's tier 2 and 3 cities hosting G20 meetings caught the most of the attention and it's remarkable. These cities were chosen for their infrastructure, connectivity and ability to accommodate international delegates, showcasing India's diverse culture and regional strengths.

India is emerging as a significant player in the MICE (Meetings, Incentives, Conferences and Exhibitions) sector due to its diverse destinations, rich cultural heritage, improved infrastructure and growing economic significance.

Diverse Destinations

Major Cities: Cities like New Delhi, Mumbai, Bengaluru, Chennai and Hyderabad are popular for hosting large-scale conferences and exhibitions. These cities offer world-class convention centers, luxury hotels and excellent connectivity.

Tourist Hotspots: Locations like Goa, Jaipur, Udaipur, Kerala and Agra provide a blend of business and leisure. These destinations are ideal for incentive travels and small to medium-sized conferences, combining work with rich cultural experiences.

Infrastructure Development

Convention Centres: India has numerous state-of-the-art convention centres such as the India International Convention and Expo Centre (IICC) in New Delhi, the Bombay Exhibition Centre (BEC) in Mumbai and the Hyderabad International Convention Centre (HICC).

Hotels: The growth of international hotel chains and high-end resorts has boosted accommodation options. Many of these hotels offer excellent conference facilities.

Transportation: Improvements in air, rail and road connectivity make travelling to and within India more convenient. Major airports have been upgraded to handle international traffic efficiently.

Economic Growth

Business Opportunities: India's growing economy attracts international businesses. Conferences and exhibitions in sectors like technology, pharmaceuticals, textiles and automotive see significant participation.

Government Initiatives: The Indian government promotes the MICE sector through various initiatives, including the Incredible India campaign and the setting up of tourism boards in states to facilitate MICE activities.

Cultural Richness

Experiential Incentives: India's cultural diversity offers unique experiences, from historical monuments and traditional arts to diverse cuisine and festivals. These elements enhance the attractiveness of incentive trips and cultural exchange programs.

Historic Venues: Many heritage sites and palaces have been converted into venues for conferences and weddings, adding a unique charm to MICE events.

Technology and Innovation

Tech Hubs: Cities like Bengaluru and Hyderabad are renowned tech hubs, making them ideal for tech conferences and exhibitions.

Smart Cities: The development of smart cities is also contributing to the growth of infrastructure conducive to MICE activities.

Supportive Services

Event Management Companies: There is a growing number of professional event management companies in India that provide comprehensive MICE services, ensuring smooth execution of events.

Catering and Hospitality: India's hospitality industry is known for its high standards, offering diverse cuisine options and exceptional service.

Challenges and Solutions

Visa and Regulatory Issues: While obtaining visas can sometimes be challenging, the Indian government has been working on streamlining the process with initiatives like e-visas for business travellers.

Language Barriers: English is widely spoken in business circles, but having multilingual support at events can further ease communication for international delegates.

Infrastructure Gaps: Continuous improvements and investments are needed in certain regions to bring them up to par with global standards.

India's potential as a MICE destination is immense, backed by its robust infrastructure, cultural appeal and economic growth. As the country continues to develop its facilities and services, it is set to become a leading destination for global MICE events.

The successful hosting of the G20 meetings has significantly bolstered India's potential as a leading MICE (Meetings, Incentives, Conferences and Exhibitions) destination. Here is a detailed analysis of how the G20 experience has enhanced India's MICE capabilities and prospects:

Enhanced Infrastructure and Facilities

Upgraded Venues: Many cities upgraded their convention centers and meeting facilities to host G20 events, leaving behind world-class venues that can now be used for future MICE activities.

Improved Connectivity: Infrastructure improvements, including better road networks, enhanced airport facilities and increased flight connectivity has made India more accessible for international business travellers.

Global Exposure and Credibility

International Recognition: Successfully hosting high-profile G20 meetings has showcased India's capability to handle large-scale international events, boosting its credibility as a reliable MICE destination.

Increased Visibility: The global attention received during the G20 presidency has increased India's visibility on the world stage, attracting potential MICE organizers.

Economic Benefits

Boost to Local Economies: Hosting G20 meetings in various cities has provided a significant economic boost to local economies through increased tourism, hospitality and related sectors.

Attraction of Future Events: The demonstrated success of G20 meetings is likely to attract other international conferences, exhibitions and corporate events to India.

Cultural and Experiential Offerings

Rich Cultural Heritage: India's diverse culture, historical landmarks and unique experiences makes it an attractive destination for incentive travel and cultural exchange programs.

Unique Venues: Historical sites and palaces, which were utilized for G20 events, offer unique and memorable venues for future MICE activities.

Government Support and Initiatives

Policy Support: Continued government initiatives and policies supporting the MICE sector will help in further developing the necessary infrastructure and services.

Ease of Doing Business: Improvements in visa processes, including e-visas and streamlined procedures for business travellers, will facilitate easier access for international delegates.

Professional Services and Expertise

Event Management: The experience gained by local event management companies during the G20 meetings enhances their ability to handle complex and large-scale MICE events.

Hospitality Industry: The hospitality industry, with its high standards of service, is well-equipped to cater to the needs of international MICE participants.

Future Prospects

Emerging Cities: Beyond the major metros, tier-2 cities that hosted G20 meetings are now on the map for potential MICE events, offering new and less explored destinations.

Technological Advancements: Cities like Bengaluru and Hyderabad, known for their tech hubs, are ideal for tech conferences and innovation-driven events, supported by state-of-the-art facilities.

India's hosting of the G20 meetings has significantly enhanced its reputation and capabilities as a MICE destination. The upgrades in infrastructure, increased global exposure and improved services position India as a prime choice for international business events. As the country continues to leverage its cultural richness, economic growth and government support, it is set to become a top-tier global MICE destination.

G20 Meeting in Srinagar

The preparations were like a whole G20 summit. Really, they were!!!

Its success was the result of meticulous planning and hard work of the officers of the Government of India, G20 Secretariat, Ministry of Tourism, Jammu and Kashmir Tourism, Ministry of Home Affairs, the Security Agencies and consulting firms (private players). Not forgetting to mention the contribution of the locals on this huge success, the people of Jammu and Kashmir were magnificent. I now understand why it is called the heaven on earth.

The G20 meeting in Srinagar had a substantial impact on Jammu and Kashmir's tourism sector, providing both immediate benefits and setting the stage for long-term growth. With continued focus on political stability, sustainable development and infrastructure maintenance, the region can capitalize on the momentum generated by the event to become a premier tourist destination.

The G20 meeting held in Srinagar, Jammu and Kashmir, had several global impacts, both in terms of geopolitics and economics. The choice of Srinagar as the venue highlighted India's strategic intentions to integrate Jammu and Kashmir more firmly into its national framework. It sent a strong message about the region's stability and potential and the geopolitical impacts of this event were evident in the followings of the global media.

The event drew significant international attention, bringing focus to the political and socio-economic situation in Jammu and Kashmir. It provided an opportunity for India to showcase its efforts toward development and normalization in the region. Hosting the G20 meeting in Srinagar facilitated high-level diplomatic engagements. It allowed for bilateral and multilateral discussions on the side-lines, enhancing India's diplomatic outreach. By successfully hosting the event, India reinforced its position on Jammu and Kashmir, countering narratives from neighbouring countries, particularly Pakistan, which claims the region. This could contribute to a recalibration of international perspectives on the territorial dispute.

The event provided an immediate economic boost to the local economy through increased demand for services, including hospitality, transport and retail. This created a ripple effect on local businesses and employment. The successful organization of the G20 meeting showcased the region's potential for future investments. It demonstrated improved infrastructure, security and stability, making it more attractive to international investors. Highlighting Jammu and Kashmir's tourism potential on a global platform has led to increased tourist inflows, promoting cultural exchange and economic growth through the tourism sector.

Discussions during the G20 meeting focused on sustainable development goals (SDGs), climate change and economic growth. The meeting underscored these themes in the context of Jammu and Kashmir, promoting sustainable practices in the region. The G20 meeting facilitated discussions on global economic policies, trade and investment, impacting global economic governance. Decisions and agreements made during the meeting can influence global markets and economies.

With a focus on digital transformation, the meeting highlighted advancements in technology and innovation. This can spur international collaborations and investments in digital infrastructure and technology sectors globally. Emphasizing climate change and environmental sustainability, the G20 meeting encouraged collective action and international cooperation on climate goals, which have far-reaching global implications. The meeting addressed post-pandemic economic recovery, discussing strategies for resilient and inclusive growth. These discussions can help shape global economic policies and recovery plans.

One Meeting and a Billion Dreams!

It was a historic G20 Meeting; it was the time when the whole world was looking at us, all the media houses were busy capturing the G20 meeting during 22nd -24th May, 2023. The Sher-i-Kashmir International Convention Centre popularly known as SKICC was converted into a "high-security facility". The serene Dal Lake overlooking the Zabarwan mountains in the backdrop was witnessing an event of this magnitude maybe for the first time in history.

The G20 meeting held in Srinagar, Jammu and Kashmir was a significant event, highlighting the region's importance and the Indian government's focus on it. The meeting brought together representatives from the world's largest economies to discuss various global economic issues. Srinagar, known for its scenic beauty and strategic importance, provided a picturesque backdrop for the discussions.

Some key points about the G20 meeting in Srinagar includes:

Agenda: The meeting focused on several critical global issues, including economic growth, sustainable development, climate change and digital transformation.

Participants: Delegates from G20 member countries attended the meeting, discussing and collaborating on policies to address pressing global challenges.

Security: Given the region's sensitive nature, extensive security measures were put in place to ensure the safety of the delegates and the smooth conduct of the event.

Local Impact: Hosting the G20 meeting in Srinagar was seen as a significant move to boost the local economy and promote tourism in Jammu and Kashmir.

Cultural Showcase: The event also provided an opportunity to showcase the rich cultural heritage and natural beauty of the region to international delegates.

The G20 meeting in Srinagar was a testament to India's commitment to fostering international cooperation and addressing global economic challenges while also promoting the development and integration of Jammu and Kashmir.

The G20 meeting in Srinagar had a notable impact on tourism in Jammu and Kashmir. Here's how it influenced the region:

Increased Visibility: The international spotlight on Srinagar during the G20 meeting brought global attention to the region's natural beauty, cultural heritage and tourism potential.

Improved Infrastructure: In preparation for the event, there were significant upgrades to local infrastructure, including roads, hotels and public amenities. These improvements benefit tourists and residents alike.

Boost to Local Economy: The influx of delegates, media and support staff provided a short-term boost to the local economy through spending on accommodation, food, transport and souvenirs.

Promotional Opportunities: The meeting provided a platform to showcase local crafts, cuisine and attractions, potentially attracting more tourists in the long term.

Enhanced Security: The heightened security measures put in place for the G20 meeting contributed to a safer environment, which can reassure tourists about the safety of the region.

Long-term Prospects

Sustained Interest: The positive exposure from the G20 meeting can lead to sustained interest in Jammu and Kashmir as a travel destination, encouraging future tourist visits.

Increased Investment: The successful hosting of such a high-profile event can attract further investment in tourism infrastructure and services, improving the overall experience for visitors.

Brand Building: The event helped in rebranding Jammu and Kashmir as a peaceful and welcoming tourist destination, overcoming previous negative perceptions due to political instability.

Challenges and Considerations

Sustainability: Ensuring that tourism development is sustainable and benefits local communities without harming the environment is crucial.

Consistency: Maintaining the improved infrastructure and security measures over the long term is necessary to keep attracting tourists.

Balanced Development: While focusing on tourism, it's important to balance development across various sectors to ensure holistic growth of the region.

The G20 meeting in Srinagar served as a catalyst for positive changes in the tourism sector, offering an opportunity for

Jammu and Kashmir to establish itself as a premier tourist destination on the global stage.

Local reactions to the G20 meeting in Srinagar, Jammu and Kashmir were mixed, reflecting a range of perspectives and sentiments within the region. Here's a detailed overview of the various reactions:

Positive Reactions

Economic Opportunities: Many local business owners and entrepreneurs welcomed the event, seeing it as an opportunity to boost the local economy. Hotels, restaurants and shops experienced increased business due to the influx of visitors.

Pride and Optimism: Some residents felt a sense of pride that their region was chosen to host such a prestigious international event. They viewed it as recognition of the region's potential and hoped it would lead to long-term benefits.

Improved Infrastructure: The infrastructure improvements made in preparation for the meeting, such as better roads, enhanced public facilities and beautification projects, were appreciated by locals who benefited from these developments.

Tourism Promotion: Local artisans, craftsmen and cultural performers saw the event as a platform to showcase their work to an international audience, potentially leading to greater recognition and business opportunities.

Critical and Cautious Reactions

Political Sentiments: Some locals were sceptical or critical of the event, viewing it through the lens of ongoing political issues in the region. They questioned whether the G20 meeting would lead to meaningful changes or merely serve as a public relations exercise.

Security Concerns: The extensive security measures, while ensuring safety, also led to inconveniences for residents. Road closures, checkpoints and heightened security protocols disrupted daily life for some locals.

Inclusive Benefits: There were concerns about whether the benefits of the event would be inclusive and reach all segments of society, particularly marginalized communities in the region.

Long-term Impact: Some residents were cautiously optimistic, waiting to see if the promised economic and infrastructural benefits would be sustained over the long term or if they would diminish once the event concluded.

Cultural and Social Reactions

Cultural Pride: The opportunity to showcase the region's rich cultural heritage, including traditional music, dance and crafts, was a source of pride for many locals. They appreciated the chance to share their culture with international delegates.

Youth Engagement: Younger residents, especially students and professionals, saw the event as an exciting opportunity to engage with global issues and gain exposure to international standards and practices.

Community Activities: Various community activities and events organized around the G20 meeting fostered a sense of community participation and engagement, with locals taking part in cultural programs, exhibitions and discussions.

The local reactions to the G20 meeting in Srinagar were diverse, reflecting a complex mix of optimism, pride, scepticism and cautious hope. While the event brought tangible benefits in terms of infrastructure and economic activity, the long-term impact on the region's development and the resolution of political issues remains to be seen.

Jammu and Kashmir lieutenant governor Manoj Sinha on addressing the Independence Day celebrations on 15 August 2023 said that foreign tourists' arrival in the region increased by 59% after the recent G20 working group meeting in Srinagar. The meeting not only strengthened political relations but also opened new possibilities in the tourism sector.

G20 Meeting and Tourism

The former Tourism Secretary Arvind Singh under whose guidance three TWG meetings were held on his address at the seminar organized by Foundation for Aviation & Sustainable Tourism (FAST) mentioned that the Indian tourism sector has an unparalleled opportunity to share its success stories on a global stage with the G20 Presidency. India is the only country which has used so many locations for G20 meetings. This shows that we have the strength to host international conferences and conventions at these places.

The G20 meeting held in Srinagar, Jammu and Kashmir had a significant impact on the region's tourism sector. Here is a detailed analysis of the potential short-term and long-term effects:

Short-term Impact

Increased Visibility: The international media coverage brought global attention to Jammu and Kashmir, highlighting its scenic beauty, cultural heritage, and tourism potential.

Immediate Boost in Tourism: The influx of delegates, media personnel and visitors during the event led to a short-term spike in hotel bookings, restaurant patronage and local tours.

Showcasing Local Culture: The G20 event included cultural programs and exhibitions that showcased local crafts, music, dance and cuisine, creating an immediate interest in the region's cultural tourism.

Infrastructure Improvements: Preparations for the G20 meeting resulted in improved infrastructure, such as better roads, upgraded public facilities and beautification projects, enhancing the overall tourist experience.

Long-term Impact

Sustained Tourism Growth: The positive exposure from the G20 meeting is expected to lead to sustained interest in Jammu and Kashmir as a travel destination, attracting more domestic and international tourists in the future.

Increased Investment: The successful hosting of such a high-profile event can attract further investment in the tourism sector, including hotels, resorts, and recreational facilities, contributing to long-term growth.

Enhanced Reputation: Hosting the G20 meeting helped rebrand Jammu and Kashmir as a safe and welcoming tourist destination, overcoming previous negative perceptions due to political instability.

Promotion of Niche Tourism: The event highlighted various niche tourism opportunities in the region, such as adventure tourism, eco-tourism, and cultural tourism, encouraging diversification of the tourism offerings.

Challenges and Considerations

Political Stability: Continued political stability and resolution of local issues are crucial to maintaining the momentum gained from the G20 meeting and ensuring sustained growth in tourism.

Sustainable Development: Ensuring that tourism development is sustainable and benefits local communities without harming the environment is essential for the long-term success of the sector.

Consistency in Infrastructure Maintenance: Maintaining and further improving the infrastructure developed for the G20 meeting is necessary to keep attracting tourists and providing a high-quality visitor experience.

Local Community Involvement: Engaging local communities in tourism development and ensuring that the benefits of increased tourism reach all segments of society are important for inclusive growth.

The G20 meeting in Srinagar had a significant global impact, enhancing India's geopolitical stance, promoting economic growth and investment in Jammu and Kashmir and contributing to global economic and policy discussions. By addressing key issues like sustainable development, climate action and digital transformation, the event underscored the importance of international cooperation in addressing global challenges.

India Tourism and Soft Power Diplomacy

The Concept of Soft Power

Soft power, a term coined by political scientist Joseph Nye in the late 20th century, refers to the ability of a country to influence others through attraction and persuasion rather than coercion or force. It stands in contrast to "hard power", which involves military force, economic sanctions, and other forms of compulsion. Soft power operates on the level of ideas, culture, diplomacy, and values, making it a crucial aspect of international relations in the modern world. This essay explores the origins, components, and implications of soft power, demonstrating its significance in shaping global dynamics.

The concept of soft power emerged as a response to the changing nature of international relations in the post-Cold War era. With the decline of direct military confrontations between superpowers, the ability to influence global affairs through non-coercive means became increasingly important. Joseph Nye introduced the term in his 1990 book **"Bound to Lead: The Changing Nature of American Power"**, where he argued that the United States, despite facing challenges from rising powers, retained a unique ability to shape global outcomes through its cultural appeal, political values, and international institutions.

Nye's idea of soft power was further elaborated in his subsequent works, particularly in *"The Paradox of American Power" (2002)* and *"Soft Power: The Means to Success in World Politics" (2004)*. He emphasized that the true strength of a nation lies not only in its military capabilities but also in its ability to attract and co-opt others, shaping their preferences through appeal rather than coercion.

Soft power is comprised of various elements that contribute to a nation's ability to attract and persuade others. These elements can be broadly categorized into three main areas: culture, political values, and foreign policy.

A nation's culture, including its arts, entertainment, and lifestyle, plays a crucial role in soft power. Hollywood movies, popular music, fashion, and cuisine are examples of how cultural exports can create a positive image of a country and make its way of life appealing to others. For instance, American culture has had a profound influence worldwide, making the United States a symbol of freedom, innovation, and modernity.

The political system and values of a nation, such as democracy, human rights and the rule of law, also contribute to its soft power. Countries that uphold and promote these values are often seen as more legitimate and morally superior, which can enhance their influence on the global stage. For example, the European Union's emphasis on human rights and democracy has bolstered its soft power, making it an attractive model for governance.

A country's foreign policy, particularly its diplomatic efforts and participation in international institutions, can enhance its soft power. Nations that engage in multilateralism, peacekeeping and humanitarian aid are often viewed more favourably and can build alliances and partnerships based on mutual respect and shared interests. The success of soft power often hinges on the perception that a country's actions align with the global good.

The significance of soft power in international relations cannot be overstated. In an increasingly interconnected world, where information and ideas flow freely across borders, the ability to influence others through attraction and persuasion is a vital tool for achieving national objectives. Soft power can help countries build alliances, resolve conflicts, and promote stability without resorting to force.

However, the use of soft power is not without challenges. The effectiveness of soft power depends on the credibility of the source and the perception of the target audience. For instance, a country that promotes democracy abroad while violating human rights at home may face accusations of hypocrisy, undermining its soft power. Additionally, soft power is often difficult to measure and quantify, making it challenging to assess its true impact.

Moreover, the rise of new global powers, such as China and India, has introduced new dynamics in the soft power landscape. These nations are increasingly investing in cultural diplomacy, media outreach and international development programs to enhance their global influence. This has led to a more competitive environment where traditional powers like the United States and Europe must adapt to maintain their soft power advantage.

Soft power is a critical concept in understanding the complexities of international relations in the 21st century. It highlights the importance of attraction, persuasion and legitimacy in achieving national objectives. While hard power remains a significant tool in the arsenal of states, the ability to influence others through non-coercive means is increasingly recognized as a key determinant of global leadership. As the world continues to evolve, the role of soft power will likely become even more central in shaping the future of international relations.

India Tourism

India's tourism industry is an essential component of its economy and a significant instrument of its soft power diplomacy. Through tourism, India projects its cultural, historical and natural wealth to the world, fostering international goodwill and enhancing its global standing.

India's tourism industry is vast and diverse, encompassing cultural, historical, medical and spiritual tourism. The country's rich heritage, marked by iconic landmarks such as the Taj Mahal, Jaipur's palaces and Kerala's backwaters, attracts millions of visitors annually. Each region of India offers a unique experience, from the snow-capped Himalayas in the north to the sun-kissed beaches of Goa in the west, the vibrant festivals of Tamil Nadu in the south and the rich tribal cultures of the northeast.

Tourism is a critical sector for India, contributing significantly to the GDP and providing employment to millions. The World Travel and Tourism Council (WTTC) reported that tourism accounted for 9.2% of India's GDP in 2019 and supported over 42 million jobs. The sector's growth stimulates other industries, such as hospitality, transportation, and handicrafts, creating a multiplier effect on the economy.

Tourism serves as a powerful tool for India's soft power diplomacy. By promoting its cultural heritage, India strengthens its cultural ties with other countries. Initiatives like the "Incredible India" campaign have been instrumental in showcasing India's cultural richness and diversity. This campaign, launched in 2002, has successfully repositioned India as a must-visit destination by highlighting its historical monuments, cuisine, art and spirituality.

India has also emerged as a hub for medical and wellness tourism, leveraging its advanced healthcare infrastructure and the traditional healing practices of Ayurveda and Yoga. Patients from across the globe visit India for affordable and high-quality medical treatments, including complex surgeries.

Simultaneously, wellness tourists seek holistic healing and rejuvenation through yoga retreats and Ayurvedic therapies. This sector not only boosts the economy but also enhances India's image as a centre for holistic health and wellness.

India's rich spiritual heritage, encompassing diverse religious traditions like Hinduism, Buddhism, Jainism and Sikhism, attracts spiritual seekers and pilgrims from around the world. Destinations like Varanasi, Bodh Gaya and Amritsar serve as significant religious and spiritual centres, fostering intercultural dialogue and understanding.

India's educational institutions, particularly in fields such as engineering, medicine and management, attract a large number of international students. By welcoming foreign students, India fosters people-to-people connections and builds long-term diplomatic relations. Initiatives like the Study in India program aim to increase the number of international students in Indian universities, further enhancing India's educational soft power.

While India's tourism industry holds immense potential, it faces several challenges, including infrastructure deficits, safety concerns and environmental sustainability. Addressing these challenges requires a concerted effort from both the government and the private sector. Investing in infrastructure, ensuring tourist safety and promoting sustainable tourism practices are essential for the industry's sustainable growth.

India's tourism industry is a vital part of its economy and a powerful tool for soft power diplomacy. By showcasing its cultural, historical, and natural treasures, India not only attracts visitors but also fosters international goodwill and strengthens its global standing. Through continuous efforts to improve infrastructure, safety and sustainability, India can harness the full potential of tourism to boost its economy and enhance its soft power influence on the global stage.

International Relations and Foreign Policy Implications

Tourism can significantly influence international relations and foreign policy. The impact of tourism on these areas can be seen in various ways, ranging from cultural exchange and economic benefits to diplomatic engagement and soft power projection. Here's how tourism interacts with and influences international relations and foreign policy:

Tourism promotes cultural exchange, allowing people from different countries to interact and understand each other's cultures, traditions and values. This exchange can foster goodwill and mutual respect, contributing to the improvement of bilateral and multilateral relations.

When tourists experience the culture, history and lifestyle of a host country, they often return with a favourable impression, which can influence perceptions back in their home country. This is a form of soft power, where a country uses its cultural appeal to attract and influence foreign publics. For instance, countries like France, Italy and Japan leverage their rich cultural heritage to attract millions of tourists, thereby enhancing their global image and influence.

Economic Interdependence and Diplomatic Relations

Tourism is a significant contributor to the economy of many countries, generating income, creating jobs, and fostering development. When two countries have a high volume of tourists traveling between them, they develop economic interdependence. This economic relationship can lead to stronger diplomatic ties, as countries may be more inclined to maintain peaceful and cooperative relations to protect their mutual economic interests.

For example, the relationship between the United States and Mexico is influenced by tourism, particularly in border regions where tourism is a key economic driver. Similarly, European countries within the Schengen Zone benefit from tourism through easier travel across borders, which strengthens regional cooperation and integration.

Diplomatic Tools and Bilateral Agreements

Tourism can be used as a diplomatic tool to improve or solidify international relations. Governments often enter into bilateral tourism agreements to facilitate travel between countries, promote mutual understanding and boost economic ties. These agreements may include visa waivers, promotional campaigns and the development of joint tourism projects.

For example, the "Tourism Diplomacy" initiative by China involves promoting Chinese culture and language through tourism, alongside developing infrastructure in Belt and Road Initiative (BRI) partner countries. This initiative serves both economic and strategic interests by strengthening ties with partner nations.

Crisis Management and Conflict Resolution

Tourism can also play a role in crisis management and conflict resolution. After conflicts or natural disasters, tourism can help rebuild a country's image and economy by attracting international visitors. This was evident in post-apartheid South Africa, where tourism helped reintegrate the country into the global community and supported its economic recovery.

In conflict resolution, tourism initiatives such as peace tourism, where people visit sites of historical conflicts to learn about them, can promote dialogue and reconciliation. These efforts can contribute to a broader understanding of peace and conflict, supporting international efforts to resolve disputes and foster stability.

Impact on Foreign Policy

The flow of tourists can influence a country's foreign policy decisions. For instance, countries that rely heavily on tourism revenue may be more inclined to pursue peaceful and cooperative foreign policies to ensure a stable environment for tourists. Conversely, countries that impose travel restrictions or sanctions on other nations may see a decline in tourism, which can impact their economy and international standing.

Additionally, tourism can serve as a platform for public diplomacy, where governments engage directly with foreign citizens. For example, nations might use international tourism events like World Expos or the Olympics to showcase their culture, technological advancements, and political values, shaping global perceptions and advancing their foreign policy objectives.

Tourism is a powerful tool that influences international relations and foreign policy in various ways. Through cultural exchange, economic interdependence, diplomatic agreements and crisis management, tourism helps shape the way countries interact with each other. It can enhance soft power, foster goodwill and create opportunities for diplomacy, making it an essential aspect of modern international relations. As global travel continues to grow, the role of tourism in shaping foreign policy and international relations is likely to become even more significant.

India's foreign policy has evolved significantly since its independence in 1947, reflecting the country's growing global stature, strategic interests, and economic aspirations. Over the years, India's approach to international relations has shifted from non-alignment during the Cold War to a more pragmatic and multi-faceted diplomacy in the 21st century. This evolution can be understood through several key phases and developments.

The Nehruvian Era (1947-1964): Non-Alignment and Idealism

India's foreign policy in the early years after independence was heavily influenced by its first Prime Minister, Jawaharlal Nehru. Nehru advocated for a policy of non-alignment, where India refused to formally align with either the United States or the Soviet Union during the Cold War. This policy was rooted in the desire to maintain sovereignty and avoid being drawn into superpower conflicts.

The Non-Aligned Movement (NAM), which India co-founded, became a cornerstone of its foreign policy, promoting peaceful coexistence, anti-colonialism, and disarmament. Nehru's emphasis on moral principles and global peace earned India a significant moral standing, particularly among newly independent nations in Asia and Africa.

Indira Gandhi and Strategic Autonomy (1966-1984)

Indira Gandhi, Nehru's daughter and successor as Prime Minister, steered India towards a more assertive and pragmatic foreign policy. The 1971 Indo-Pakistan War, which led to the creation of Bangladesh, marked a turning point in India's foreign relations. During this period, India signed the Treaty of Peace, Friendship and Cooperation with the Soviet Union, signalling a tilt towards Moscow, albeit without completely abandoning non-alignment.

India also pursued nuclear capability during this period, culminating in the 1974 "Smiling Buddha" nuclear test. This move was driven by the need for strategic autonomy and deterrence, particularly in the context of China's nuclear capabilities and the perceived unreliability of international guarantees.

Economic Liberalization and Global Integration (1991-Present)

The end of the Cold War and the economic crisis of 1991 led India to liberalize its economy and integrate more closely with the global market. This shift had profound implications for its foreign policy. Under Prime Ministers P.V. Narasimha Rao and Atal Bihari Vajpayee, India began to prioritize economic diplomacy, seeking to attract foreign investment and technology while expanding trade relations.

India's "Look East Policy" was launched in the 1990s to enhance economic and strategic ties with Southeast Asia. This policy evolved into the "Act East Policy" under Prime Minister Narendra Modi, reflecting a more proactive engagement with the region. India also normalized relations with the United States, culminating in the 2005 U.S.-India Civil Nuclear Agreement, which marked a significant shift in bilateral relations.

India as an Emerging Global Power (2000s-Present)

In the 21st century, India's foreign policy has increasingly reflected its aspirations as a rising global power. India has sought a more prominent role in global governance, advocating for reforms in international institutions like the United Nations Security Council (UNSC), where it seeks a permanent seat.

India has also strengthened its strategic partnerships with major powers, including the United States, Russia, Japan, and the European Union, while deepening ties with neighbouring countries through regional organizations like the South Asian Association for Regional Cooperation (SAARC) and the Bay of Bengal Initiative for Multi-Sectoral Technical and Economic Cooperation (BIMSTEC).

The strategic relationship with the United States, particularly under the Modi government, has expanded into areas like defence, counterterrorism, and technology, with initiatives like the Quad (Quadrilateral Security Dialogue) bringing together India, the U.S., Japan, and Australia to address security challenges in the Indo-Pacific region.

Balancing Act in a Multipolar World

In recent years, India's foreign policy has been characterized by a balancing act between major global powers while advancing its strategic interests. India maintains strong ties with Russia, especially in defence, while simultaneously deepening its partnership with the U.S. India has also worked to manage its complex relationship with China, marked by both cooperation and competition, particularly in the wake of border tensions.

India's approach to multilateralism has also been pragmatic, participating actively in forums like the G20, BRICS and the Shanghai Cooperation Organization (SCO). These platforms allow India to collaborate on global issues like climate change, trade and terrorism while asserting its interests on the global stage.

Neighbourhood First and Regional Leadership

India's "Neighbourhood First" policy emphasizes building strong relationships with its South Asian neighbours, recognizing that a stable and prosperous neighbourhood is vital for its own security and economic growth. India has provided developmental assistance, infrastructure investments and humanitarian aid to countries like Afghanistan, Nepal, Bhutan and Sri Lanka, positioning itself as a regional leader.

However, India faces challenges in its neighbourhood, particularly with Pakistan and China. The longstanding conflict with Pakistan over Kashmir and the recent border clashes with China in the Galwan Valley has tested India's diplomatic and military strategies.

India's foreign policy has flourished over the years, evolving from the idealism of non-alignment to a more pragmatic and multi-dimensional approach. Today, India is recognized as an emerging global power with a growing influence on international affairs. Its foreign policy reflects a balance between strategic autonomy, economic interests, and global responsibilities. As India continues to navigate a complex and multipolar world, its ability to adapt and assert its interests will be crucial in shaping its future role on the global stage.

India as 'Voice of the Global South'

India's role as a voice of the Global South has been a central theme in its foreign policy, especially as it has sought to assert itself as a leading advocate for developing nations in global forums and G20 was one such. The term "Global South" generally refers to countries in Africa, Latin America, Asia and Oceania that share common challenges, such as poverty, underdevelopment and the legacy of colonialism. These nations often seek greater equity in the global system, which is dominated by wealthier, industrialized countries of the Global North.

Historical Roots and Non-Alignment

India's role as a representative of the Global South has deep historical roots, dating back to its leadership in the Non-Aligned Movement (NAM) during the Cold War. Founded in 1961, NAM was an initiative by newly independent countries, including India, to avoid aligning with either the United States or the Soviet Union, the two superpowers at the time. India, under the leadership of Prime Minister Jawaharlal Nehru, played a key role in establishing NAM as a platform for countries of the Global South to express their collective concerns and aspirations.

NAM allowed India to champion the principles of sovereignty, self-determination, and anti-colonialism, positioning itself as a leader among developing nations. India's leadership in NAM reinforced its commitment to advocating for the rights and interests of the Global South, a role that it continues to emphasize in various international arenas.

Economic Diplomacy and South-South Cooperation

In the post-Cold War era, as the global economy became increasingly interconnected, India adapted its approach to focus on economic diplomacy and South-South cooperation. This shift was driven by India's economic liberalization in the early 1990s, which opened new opportunities for trade, investment and technological collaboration with other developing countries.

India has actively promoted South-South cooperation to foster economic growth, reduce dependence on the Global North and address common challenges such as poverty, inequality and sustainable development. Initiatives like the India-Africa Forum Summit and the India-Brazil-South Africa (IBSA) Dialogue Forum are examples of India's efforts to strengthen ties with other Global South nations through trade, technology transfer and capacity-building.

India has also been a key player in the BRICS group (Brazil, Russia, India, China, and South Africa), which was formed to represent the interests of emerging economies and challenge the dominance of Western institutions like the International Monetary Fund (IMF) and the World Bank. Through BRICS, India has advocated for reforms in global financial governance and sought to create alternative mechanisms, such as the New Development Bank (NDB), to support infrastructure and development projects in the Global South.

Climate Change and Global Governance

As a voice of the Global South, India has taken a proactive stance on issues of global governance, particularly in the areas of climate change and sustainable development. India has consistently argued that developed countries, which have historically contributed the most to greenhouse gas emissions, should bear a greater responsibility in addressing climate change. This position aligns with the principle of "common but differentiated responsibilities" (CBDR), which India has championed in international climate negotiations.

At the 2015 Paris Climate Conference (COP21), India played a crucial role in securing a global agreement that recognized the need for climate justice and financial support for developing countries to transition to a low-carbon economy. India's leadership in the International Solar Alliance (ISA), a coalition of solar-rich countries, further exemplifies its commitment to promoting renewable energy solutions that benefit the Global South.

Strategic Autonomy and Multilateralism

India's foreign policy has emphasized strategic autonomy, allowing it to pursue an independent course that aligns with the interests of the Global South. This approach has been evident in India's participation in multilateral institutions, where it has consistently advocated for the reform of global governance structures to better reflect the realities of the 21st century.

India has called for the expansion of the United Nations Security Council (UNSC) to include more representation from developing countries, arguing that the current structure is outdated and does not reflect the diversity of the global community. As part of the G20, India has also pushed for greater inclusivity and the prioritization of development issues that are critical to the Global South, such as poverty reduction, food security and access to technology.

Humanitarian Assistance and Development Aid

India has increasingly positioned itself as a provider of humanitarian assistance and development aid to countries in need, particularly in the Global South. Through its development partnerships, India has offered technical assistance, infrastructure projects and capacity-building programs to countries in Africa, Southeast Asia, and the Pacific Islands.

India's humanitarian efforts are often characterized by a focus on "development cooperation," rather than aid in the traditional sense, reflecting a partnership approach that emphasizes mutual benefit and respect for sovereignty. For example, India's assistance to Afghanistan in areas like education, healthcare and infrastructure has been framed as part of a broader commitment to helping the country rebuild after decades of conflict.

The COVID-19 Pandemic and Vaccine Diplomacy

The COVID-19 pandemic provided an opportunity for India to reinforce its role as a leader of the Global South through its vaccine diplomacy. India emerged as a major producer and supplier of COVID-19 vaccines, launching the "Vaccine Maitri" (Vaccine Friendship) initiative to provide vaccines to over 90 countries, many of them in the Global South. This effort not only showcased India's capacity to contribute to global health but also strengthened its ties with countries in Africa, Latin America and Asia.

India's vaccine diplomacy underscored its commitment to addressing global inequalities and its ability to act as a responsible and capable partner in times of crisis. This initiative also aligned with India's broader foreign policy goals of enhancing its soft power and deepening its engagement with the Global South.

India's role as a voice of the Global South has been a consistent and evolving aspect of its foreign policy, rooted in its historical leadership in the Non-Aligned Movement and extending to its current efforts in promoting South-South cooperation, climate justice and global governance reform. Through its advocacy in multilateral forums, economic diplomacy and humanitarian initiatives, India has sought to represent the interests and aspirations of developing countries on the global stage.

As India continues to rise as a global power, its ability to champion the causes of the Global South while navigating complex geopolitical dynamics will be crucial in shaping its future role in international affairs. India's commitment to strategic autonomy, inclusivity and sustainable development will likely remain key pillars of its foreign policy as it seeks to balance its national interests with its responsibilities as a leader of the Global South.

The increasing geostrategic and political instability in Asia is a critical issue that has profound implications for regional and global security. Asia, home to several of the world's largest and most populous nations, is experiencing a range of conflicts, power struggles and territorial disputes that are contributing to a volatile security environment. This instability is shaped by several key factors, including great power rivalry, territorial disputes, nationalist movements and non-state actors. Below, I explore some of the major sources of instability in the region.

Great Power Rivalry: The U.S.-China Strategic Competition

The strategic rivalry between the United States and China is one of the most significant sources of instability in Asia. As China rises as a global power, it has increasingly asserted its influence in the Asia-Pacific region, challenging the U.S.-led order that has prevailed since the end of World War II. This competition is evident in several areas:

South China Sea Disputes: China's assertive claims over the South China Sea, backed by military build-up and the creation of artificial islands, have heightened tensions with neighbouring countries, including Vietnam, the Philippines and Malaysia. The U.S., which supports freedom of navigation in international waters, has conducted freedom of navigation operations (FONOPs) in the region, leading to frequent confrontations with Chinese forces.

Taiwan Strait Tensions: The status of Taiwan is a major flashpoint in U.S.-China relations. China views Taiwan as a breakaway province and has not ruled out the use of force to achieve reunification. The U.S. supports Taiwan's self-defence capabilities, leading to a delicate and potentially explosive situation. Recent military drills by China near Taiwan and U.S. arms sales to Taiwan have further exacerbated tensions.

Technological and Economic Rivalry: The U.S.-China competition extends beyond military and strategic realms to include economic and technological domains. The rivalry over 5G technology, trade tariffs and economic sanctions has contributed to a decoupling in critical sectors, increasing the risk of economic instability and strategic miscalculations.

Territorial Disputes and Nationalism: Asia is home to numerous territorial disputes, many of which are fuelled by historical grievances, nationalism, and competition for resources. These disputes contribute to regional instability and have the potential to escalate into armed conflict:

India-China Border Dispute: The longstanding border dispute between India and China has seen periodic flare-ups, the most significant being the 2020 Galwan Valley clash in which soldiers from both sides were killed. The Line of Actual Control (LAC) remains a volatile flashpoint, with both countries increasing their military presence in the region.

Korean Peninsula: The Korean Peninsula remains a major source of instability in Northeast Asia. North Korea's nuclear weapons program and its occasional provocations, such as missile tests and cyberattacks, contribute to regional tensions. The lack of progress in denuclearization talks has kept the peninsula on edge, with the potential for renewed conflict.

Senkaku/Diaoyu Islands Dispute: The Senkaku Islands (known as Diaoyu in China) are a group of uninhabited islets in the East China Sea that are claimed by both Japan and China. The dispute has led to confrontations between Japanese and Chinese coast guard vessels and nationalist sentiments in both countries have exacerbated the situation.

Nationalism and Identity Politics: Nationalism and identity politics are on the rise across Asia, fuelling internal and external conflicts. In many cases, governments have used nationalist rhetoric to consolidate power, but this has also led to greater regional tensions.

Non-State Actors and Transnational Threats: Non-state actors, including terrorist groups and insurgent movements, contribute to instability across Asia. These groups often exploit weak governance, social grievances, and ethnic tensions to further their agendas:

Terrorism in South Asia: Terrorist groups such as the Taliban in Afghanistan, Lashkar-e-Taiba in Pakistan and ISIS affiliates in Southeast Asia continue to pose significant threats to regional security. The resurgence of the Taliban in Afghanistan following the U.S. withdrawal in 2021 has led to concerns about the country becoming a safe haven for global terrorist networks.

Piracy and Maritime Security: Piracy, particularly in Southeast Asia, remains a threat to maritime security. The Strait of Malacca, a critical chokepoint for global trade, has seen periodic piracy incidents, threatening shipping and regional stability.

Cybersecurity Threats: The rise of cyberattacks by state and non-state actors in Asia has added a new dimension to regional instability. Countries like China, North Korea and Iran have been accused of carrying out cyber operations against other nations, targeting critical infrastructure, financial systems and government institutions.

Economic and Environmental Challenges: Economic inequality, resource scarcity and environmental challenges such as climate change are also contributing to instability in Asia. The competition for natural resources, such as water and energy, has the potential to exacerbate existing conflicts:

Water Disputes: Asia is home to several major rivers which crosses national boundaries, leading to disputes over water usage and management. The Mekong River dispute involving China and Southeast Asian nations and the Indus Water Treaty tensions between India and Pakistan, are examples of how water scarcity can fuel regional tensions.

Climate Change and Migration: Climate change is increasingly becoming a security threat in Asia, with rising sea levels, extreme weather events and desertification leading to displacement and migration. These environmental challenges are likely to exacerbate existing conflicts over resources and territory.

The increasing geostrategic and political instability in Asia is driven by a complex interplay of factors, including great power rivalry, territorial disputes, nationalism, non-state actors and environmental challenges. As Asia continues to rise in global importance, the region's instability poses significant risks not only to regional security but also to global peace and economic stability.

Managing these challenges will require effective diplomacy, conflict resolution mechanisms and regional cooperation. The role of multilateral organizations like ASEAN, the Shanghai Cooperation Organization (SCO) and the United Nations will be crucial in addressing these issues. Additionally, the major powers, particularly the U.S. and China, will need to find ways to manage their competition and avoid escalation, as their actions will significantly shape the future stability of the region. India is an important player in Asia and its role will be crucial in defining the geostrategic positioning of states in this coveted region.

India's G20 Presidency! People's G20 Presidency!

India's G20 Presidency in 2023, often termed as the "People's G20 Presidency", reflected an effort to make global governance accessible and relatable to the masses, both in India and around the world. This chapter explains how India made it possible.

Extensive National Engagement:

Broad Geographic Reach: G20-related events were not limited to New Delhi or major metropolitan hubs but spread across 50 Indian cities, from Kashmir to Kerala. This decentralized hosting allowed a diverse range of citizens to participate, making the G20 a national event.

Involvement of Local Communities: Local artisans, cultural groups and businesses were integrated into G20 events. This not only showcased India's cultural heritage but also economically benefited small and local businesses, contributing to the idea of a grassroots-level impact.

Academic and Youth Participation: Special engagement groups such as the "Y20" (Youth 20) and "S20" (Science 20) were created to involve students, researchers, and young professionals. Universities across India hosted discussions and summits focused on issues ranging from climate change to entrepreneurship.

Themes and Priorities of the G20 Presidency:

India's G20 presidency adopted themes and priorities that directly resonated with both its domestic and global populations, focusing on real-world challenges faced by billions:

Digital Public Infrastructure: India showcased its success with digital tools like Aadhaar (biometric ID system), UPI (Unified Payments Interface) and its rapid digital transformation during the pandemic. This focus resonated with developing countries looking for scalable, low-cost digital solutions.

Green Development and Lifestyle for Environment (LiFE): This initiative encouraged sustainable living, with a focus on individual and collective climate action. India presented its leadership on issues like renewable energy (e.g., the International Solar Alliance) and low-carbon lifestyles.

Health and Pandemic Preparedness: Post-COVID-19, health security and pandemic preparedness were key agenda points. India's G20 presidency promoted equitable vaccine distribution, with an emphasis on strengthening global health systems and creating more resilient global supply chains.

Global South and Development-Centric Approach:

Voice of the Global South: India positioned itself as a representative of the developing world during its G20 presidency, emphasizing the unique challenges and perspectives of Global South nations. This involved addressing issues like:

- Debt restructuring for developing countries.

- Fair access to resources like technology and climate financing.

- Ensuring that global decisions reflect the priorities of low-income and emerging economies.

Hosting the Global South Summit: In early 2023, India held a special "Voice of Global South" summit ahead of the G20 meetings, allowing non-G20 countries, especially those from Africa, Asia and Latin America, to express their concerns. This ensured that their priorities would be reflected in G20 deliberations.

Technology and Digital Platforms for Public Participation:

Digital Outreach and Engagement: India's presidency made extensive use of social media, online town halls and webinars to involve the public in discussions. This tech-enabled approach allowed people to interact with G20 themes, leaders and outcomes, bringing greater transparency.

MyGov Platform: The Indian government's MyGov platform, a participatory governance tool, was actively used to solicit ideas from citizens. Campaigns, quizzes, and contests on G20 themes were launched to generate public interest and involvement.

Innovative Applications: India launched a mobile app for the G20, which allowed users to track events, access documents and stay updated on the presidency's progress. This app was available to the global public, further supporting transparency.

Cultural Diplomacy and Showcasing India's Heritage:

Cultural Performances: G20 meetings were often accompanied by performances highlighting India's traditional music, dance and folk art. This soft diplomacy helped create a connection between international delegates and India's rich cultural history.

Cultural Showcases: Local arts and crafts from different Indian states were promoted through exhibitions, gifting of artisanal products and showcasing India's crafts through specially designed G20 souvenirs. This was in line with promoting India's "Make in India" and *"Aatmanirbhar Bharat"* (self-reliant India) initiatives.

G20 Summit Design: The design and branding of the G20 summit incorporated traditional Indian elements like the lotus (a symbol of spirituality and purity), further embedding India's cultural identity into the presidency.

Cross-Sectoral Stakeholder Engagement:

Civil Society and Think Tanks: India encouraged the participation of civil society organizations and think tanks, especially through the Civil 20 (C20) and Think 20 (T20) groups. These platforms fostered discussions on socio-economic challenges, human rights and sustainable development, allowing various interest groups to contribute to G20 policy discussions.

Business and Economic Focus: The Business 20 (B20) platform saw heightened involvement of Indian and international businesses. This led to discussions on inclusive global growth, innovation, and the need for sustainable business practices, particularly emphasizing small and medium enterprises (SMEs).

Legacy and Long-Term Impact:

India's G20 presidency was designed not just as a one-time event but as part of a larger vision of global leadership and participation. Some potential long-term impacts include:

Shifting Global Governance Narratives: India used the presidency to argue for reforms in global institutions like the World Trade Organization (WTO), World Bank and International Monetary Fund (IMF), emphasizing the need for a more balanced and inclusive global order.

Post-G20 Initiatives: India's focus on digital public goods, health preparedness and climate finance during the G20 could pave the way for new multilateral initiatives in these areas, giving India a continued role in shaping global policies.

Public-Private Partnerships: India's G20 presidency promoted the idea of Public-Private Partnerships (PPP) to solve global challenges. Several Indian businesses were involved in events related to climate action, digital innovation, and sustainable infrastructure development, bringing the private sector into the broader G20 agenda.

By making the G20 presidency a "people's presidency," India succeeded in breaking the stereotype of G20 summits being elite gatherings disconnected from ordinary citizens. This approach not only amplified the voices of diverse stakeholders but also highlighted India's role as a responsible and inclusive global leader. The presidency strengthened India's global diplomatic footprint, creating a legacy of inclusivity, innovation, and leadership.

The Global Impact

India's G20 Presidency in 2023 was globally significant, as it marked the country's emergence as a major player in global governance and diplomacy. The world's response, including from the West and other regions, was largely positive, with several key highlights in how different regions perceived India's role.

1. Western Response: Support and Strategic Interest:

a. United States:

The U.S. viewed India's G20 presidency as a strategic opportunity to further enhance its partnership with India, a cornerstone of its Indo-Pacific strategy. The U.S. welcomed India's leadership on issues like climate change, digital infrastructure, and global economic reforms. The Biden administration frequently expressed support for India's presidency, seeing it as aligned with shared values like democracy, pluralism, and open markets.

Key themes of cooperation included:

Climate Change and Green Energy: The U.S. and India worked closely on sustainable energy and green technologies, an area the U.S. highlighted as a priority during India's G20 term.

Technology and Digital Economy: India's push for a digital public infrastructure framework, which highlighted the country's success with platforms like UPI (Unified Payments

Interface), was appreciated by Western nations, particularly the U.S. and the EU.

b. European Union (EU):

The EU strongly supported India's G20 presidency, especially its focus on global economic stability and multilateralism. The EU saw India as a critical partner in addressing global challenges like inflation, climate action and the need for multilateral reforms. There was also significant emphasis on green growth, where the EU applauded India's commitment to sustainable development and its leadership in initiatives like the International Solar Alliance.

The European perspective on India's G20 presidency emphasized:

Trade and Investment: The EU appreciated India's facilitation of trade talks and economic cooperation during its G20 leadership.

Global South Representation: The EU acknowledged India's efforts to represent the Global South, especially at a time when emerging economies needed stronger global representation in forums like the G20.

c. United Kingdom:

The UK, under the leadership of Rishi Sunak, was especially supportive of India's presidency. The historic ties between the two countries, along with shared goals of economic development and strategic security in the Indo-Pacific, resulted in a close alignment of interests. The UK also recognized India's role in championing the concerns of the developing world and its advocacy for reforming global financial institutions to be more inclusive.

2. Response from Other Parts of the World

a. Global South:

India positioned itself as a voice for the Global South during its G20 presidency, focusing on issues like debt relief, food and energy security and global inequality. This resonated strongly with many countries in Africa, Latin America and Southeast Asia, who appreciated India's efforts to bring attention to their needs on the global stage.

Key points in the Global South's response included:

Debt Relief and Financing: India highlighted the challenges many developing countries faced in repaying debts, pushing for reforms in international financial institutions like the IMF and the World Bank.

Food and Energy Security: India advocated for more robust supply chains and international cooperation to ensure food security; a major issue exacerbated by the Russia-Ukraine conflict.

Several African and Latin American countries expressed their gratitude for India's leadership in representing their concerns at the G20, enhancing India's image as a global mediator between the developed and developing worlds.

b. China:

China's response to India's G20 presidency was mixed. While China participated in G20 discussions, there was underlying geopolitical tension due to border disputes and India's growing strategic alignment with the U.S. and its allies. India's focus on sovereignty, regional stability and leadership in the Indo-Pacific drew cautious reactions from Beijing. Despite these tensions, China acknowledged India's role in addressing global economic challenges but remained wary of India's increasing influence on the world stage.

c. Russia:

India maintained a balanced approach to Russia during its G20 presidency, managing to avoid aligning itself overtly with either side in the context of the Russia-Ukraine war. This neutrality was seen as a diplomatic success, allowing India to maintain relations with Russia while also engaging with Western nations. Russia appreciated India's stance, which focused on multilateralism and economic issues rather than direct political confrontation over the Ukraine crisis.

d. Middle East:

Countries in the Middle East, particularly the Gulf Cooperation Council (GCC) members, viewed India's presidency favourably due to the strong economic ties between India and the region. The Middle East appreciated India's inclusive approach to energy transition, sustainable development and fostering peace and stability. India's role in securing agreements on energy cooperation, especially regarding oil and gas, was viewed positively.

3. Key Themes of India's Global Leadership

a. Digital Public Infrastructure and Technology:

India's promotion of digital public infrastructure as a tool for inclusive growth was widely praised, particularly by nations in the West and emerging economies. India's success in deploying technologies that facilitate financial inclusion, healthcare and governance was seen as a model for other countries.

b. Focus on the Global South:

India's presidency was marked by a distinct focus on the needs and concerns of the Global South. This was evident in India's leadership on food security, healthcare and efforts to reform global governance structures to give more representation to developing countries.

c. Climate Change and Sustainability:

India positioned itself as a leader in sustainable development, with a strong emphasis on renewable energy and climate action. Initiatives like the "LiFE" (Lifestyle for Environment) movement were designed to inspire climate-friendly practices globally. Western nations, particularly in the EU, applauded these efforts, as they aligned with global goals for carbon reduction and sustainability.

4. Global Perception of India's Diplomatic Balancing Act

India's ability to maintain a neutral stance on contentious global issues, such as the Russia-Ukraine war, while continuing to advocate for economic cooperation and development was seen as a diplomatic strength. India was able to host a successful G20 summit that included both Western nations and countries with differing political views, such as Russia and China, demonstrating India's capability to act as a bridge-builder in an increasingly polarized world.

Conclusion: A Respected Global Leader

India's G20 presidency was widely perceived as a success, with the country emerging as a key player in global diplomacy. The West appreciated India's focus on sustainability, digital innovation, and global cooperation. Meanwhile, the Global South valued India's advocacy for their needs on the international stage. Overall, India was seen as a nation capable of navigating complex geopolitical landscapes while pushing for inclusive, multilateral solutions to global challenges.

India's ability to manage diverse interests, facilitate meaningful discussions and champion development goals solidified its reputation as a global leader, especially at a time when the world was grappling with economic uncertainties and geopolitical tensions.

Geopolitical Ambitions Through G20 Presidency

India's G20 Presidency in 2023 was not just an opportunity to lead the world's most powerful economies but also a platform to assert its growing geopolitical influence. By leveraging the G20 platform, India sought to reshape global governance, project itself as a leader of the Global South and reinforce its strategic vision in a multipolar world. Here is an in-depth look at how India used the G20 to advance its geopolitical ambitions.

Positioning as a Global Power: India's G20 Presidency marked its growing stature in global politics. By hosting the world's largest economies, India reinforced its position as a rising power capable of shaping the international agenda. The G20 presidency allowed India to showcase its strengths in areas like economic management, technological innovation, and sustainable development, all while pushing for reforms in global governance.

Showcasing Economic Strength: As one of the fastest-growing economies, India projected itself as an emerging global economic powerhouse. India used the G20 platform to emphasize its leadership in areas like digital infrastructure, financial inclusion, and green energy. Initiatives such as promoting "Digital Public Infrastructure (DPI)" — which highlighted India's success with UPI and other digital governance models — allowed India to position itself as a leader in the global digital economy, especially for developing nations.

Promoting Multilateralism: India advocated for a more multipolar world, where the balance of power is distributed among multiple centres of influence. In this context, India's G20 Presidency focused on building a "multipolar global order", where developing nations have a stronger voice in shaping global governance structures like the United Nations, the World Bank, and the IMF.

Championing the Global South: One of India's primary ambitions during its G20 presidency was to position itself as the voice and advocate for the "Global South". This was evident in India's emphasis on the issues faced by developing nations, including debt relief, climate financing, food security and equitable access to technology and vaccines.

Addressing Debt Distress: India made global debt relief for developing nations a core issue during its presidency, pushing for multilateral financial institutions to create mechanisms that ease the financial burden on indebted nations. This focus allowed India to portray itself as a champion of developing economies, especially in Africa, Latin America, and Southeast Asia.

Food and Energy Security: India used its presidency to highlight the vulnerabilities in global food and energy supply chains, exacerbated by the COVID-19 pandemic and the Russia-Ukraine conflict. By advocating for secure and equitable access to these critical resources, India aligned its interests with those of the Global South, while also building alliances with nations facing similar challenges. India's role as a mediator in promoting food security initiatives and ensuring global supply chain resilience elevated its diplomatic standing with many nations across Asia, Africa, and Latin America.

Reform of Global Governance

India's G20 Presidency echoed the demand for reforming global institutions, such as the United Nations, the World Bank and the IMF. India argued that these institutions, created in the post-World War II era, no longer reflected the realities of today's world, particularly the rise of emerging economies and the Global South. India called for reforms that would provide greater representation and voting rights to developing nations in these institutions, aligning itself with the broader agenda of global equity and justice.

Advancing Strategic Interests in the Indo-Pacific

The Indo-Pacific region was a key focus of India's geopolitical strategy during the G20 Presidency. As India seeks to establish itself as a dominant player in the Indo-Pacific, it used the G20 platform to advance its regional influence and promote stability in the area.

Countering China's Influence

India's G20 presidency allowed it to subtly counterbalance China's growing influence in the Indo-Pacific. While India maintained diplomatic engagements with China during the G20 meetings, it simultaneously used the platform to strengthen its partnerships with other regional powers, such as the U.S., Japan and Australia, under the Quad framework. India's advocacy for a "free, open and rules-based Indo-Pacific" resonated with Western nations, which are wary of China's assertiveness in the region.

Strategic Partnerships

India deepened its partnerships with key Indo-Pacific nations during its presidency. By hosting high-level meetings with the U.S., Japan and Australia, India demonstrated its commitment to fostering strategic ties and promoting regional security. The

G20 was a stage for India to align its strategic interests with like-minded countries, ensuring that the Indo-Pacific remains a region of cooperation, not confrontation.

Climate Diplomacy and Green Leadership

India's leadership on climate change and green energy was a cornerstone of its geopolitical ambitions during the G20. Recognizing the global urgency of climate action, India used its presidency to assert its role as a leader in sustainable development and green energy transition.

International Solar Alliance and Green Financing

India pushed for increased global financing for climate adaptation and mitigation, particularly for developing countries that are disproportionately affected by climate change. The International Solar Alliance (ISA), an initiative led by India to promote solar energy across the world, gained further momentum under India's G20 presidency, as it sought to position itself as a key player in the global renewable energy transition.

India also advocated for climate justice, emphasizing that the responsibility of tackling climate change should be shared equitably, with developed nations providing more support to developing countries.

Diplomatic Balancing Act: Navigating Global Tensions

India's G20 Presidency coincided with a period of heightened global tensions, particularly due to the Russia-Ukraine conflict and the U.S.-China rivalry. India's ability to maintain a balanced diplomatic stance while navigating these tensions demonstrated its geopolitical maturity and ambition to play the role of a "global mediator".

Neutral Stance on the Russia-Ukraine War

India's stance on the Russia-Ukraine conflict, while maintaining neutrality, allowed it to act as a bridge between the West and Russia. India refrained from overtly criticizing Russia, given its historical ties and energy dependence, but also remained engaged with the West, advocating for dialogue and peaceful resolutions. This balancing act underscored India's ambition to be seen as an independent power capable of mediating between conflicting parties.

Engaging with China

While border tensions with China continued, India maintained diplomatic engagements with Beijing during the G20. India's strategic ambiguity — cooperating on global economic issues while standing firm on its territorial sovereignty — was a calculated move to balance regional power dynamics. This pragmatic approach allowed India to avoid direct confrontation while advancing its regional and global interests.

Promoting India as a Cultural and Civilizational Power

India also used its G20 presidency to project it's "soft power" emphasizing its cultural heritage, pluralism and democratic values. By promoting themes of "Vasudhaiva Kutumbakam" (The World is One Family) and highlighting India's ancient civilizational ethos of inclusivity, India presented itself as a model for diverse, democratic, and multicultural societies. Cultural diplomacy played a significant role in building India's image as a country that bridges the past with the future, offering lessons in coexistence, peace, and development.

India's G20 Presidency in 2023 was a pivotal moment in the country's geopolitical trajectory. Through its leadership, India not only amplified its voice on the world stage but also advanced its ambitions of becoming a key player in global governance. By positioning itself as the voice of the Global South, advocating for a rules-based Indo-Pacific, pushing for global financial reforms, and leading on climate action, India showcased its ability to navigate complex global challenges while shaping a more multipolar and inclusive world order.

The G20 presidency demonstrated that India is not just a regional power but a global player with the ambition to influence international decision-making, promote multilateralism and act as a bridge between developed and developing nations.

Youth and their Emerging Role in Foreign Policy

In recent years, India's youth have increasingly become involved in foreign policy discussions, marking a significant shift in the nation's approach to global engagement. The past decade has seen a transformation in how foreign policy is perceived, with a notable rise in youth participation in diplomatic affairs. This transformation has been driven by India's increasing global presence and the emphasis on platforms such as the G20, which has opened new avenues for young leaders to contribute to global discourse. In this chapter, we will explore how India's youth are engaging in foreign policy, the changing perceptions of diplomacy over the last decade and the pivotal role the G20 has played in fostering this engagement.

The Traditional View of Foreign Policy in India

Historically, foreign policy was seen as a realm exclusive to seasoned diplomats, bureaucrats, and political elites in India. Young people were often side-lined in discussions about diplomacy and international relations, with limited access to platforms where they could voice their opinions. Foreign policy was largely viewed as a complex, state-centric process concerned with security, trade, and bilateral relations, with little room for youth engagement or public discourse.

This traditional perception of foreign policy as an exclusive domain began to shift as globalization accelerated and India became more integrated into the global economy. The role of the state in international affairs started to expand beyond hard diplomacy, creating new opportunities for civil society, academia, and young professionals to participate in global governance.

The Decade of Transformation: 2010–2020

The decade from 2010 to 2020 has been a period of unprecedented change for India in terms of its foreign policy outlook. Several factors contributed to this transformation, including:

1. Globalization and Digital Connectivity: The spread of information technology and social media made foreign policy issues more accessible to the general public, including young people. Topics such as climate change, human rights and economic development became widely discussed on digital platforms, attracting the attention of India's youth. Youth-driven movements, both local and global, began influencing political agendas and foreign policy decisions.

2. India's Economic Growth and Global Standing: As India's economy grew, so did its importance on the global stage. This newfound prominence increased youth interest in understanding how India's international relations were shaping its development. A growing middle class and increased access to education meant that more young people were studying international relations and looking to make a career in diplomacy or global affairs.

3. Educational Opportunities and Exchanges: Over the past decade, there has been a rise in programs focused on international studies, foreign policy, and diplomacy in Indian universities. Educational exchanges and scholarships, such as the Chevening Scholarship and the Fulbright Program, have encouraged Indian students to study abroad, further exposing them to global politics and diplomacy. These experiences

brought back diverse perspectives and built a generation of globally aware youth leaders.

4. Youth-Led Organizations and Diplomacy Forums: Youth-led organizations such as the Indian Youth Diplomacy Forum (IYDF) and international programs like the Model United Nations (MUN) have empowered students and young professionals to simulate diplomatic processes, engage in policy discussions and understand global governance issues first-hand. These forums also acted as incubators for young people aspiring to influence foreign policy decisions.

Changing Perceptions of Foreign Policy

In the past decade, Indian youth have moved from being passive observers of foreign policy to active participants. This shift in perception can be attributed to the realization that foreign policy has tangible effects on domestic issues, such as employment, environmental sustainability, and national security. As a result, there has been growing interest in global governance, multilateralism, and regional cooperation.

1. Issue-Based Diplomacy: The growing importance of cross-border issues such as climate change, cybersecurity, global health (particularly during the COVID-19 pandemic) and human rights has resonated deeply with India's youth. Many of these issues directly affect their futures, leading them to become more engaged in discussions on how India should navigate these challenges. Climate diplomacy, in particular, has galvanized youth participation, with India's young climate activists playing an active role in shaping the nation's stance in international forums.

2. Soft Power Diplomacy: India's emphasis on soft power, particularly through cultural diplomacy, yoga, Bollywood and the promotion of the Indian diaspora, has also changed how young people perceive the country's foreign policy. Youth-led

cultural exchange programs, digital diplomacy and public diplomacy initiatives have created opportunities for young Indians to represent their country on global platforms, leveraging India's rich cultural heritage to foster international goodwill.

3. Public Diplomacy and Youth Leadership: The Indian government has increasingly recognized the potential of youth in contributing to foreign policy discussions. Initiatives such as the Ministry of External Affairs' Public Diplomacy Division and various outreach programs have made efforts to include youth voices in shaping India's image abroad. Young leaders are now seen as important actors in diplomacy, as they bring innovative perspectives and can act as bridges between nations.

The Role of the G20 in Youth Engagement

One of the most significant platforms for youth engagement in foreign policy has been the G20. India's involvement in the G20 process has not only enhanced its global stature but also created opportunities for youth to engage with world leaders and influence international policy. The G20 Youth Summits and related activities have been instrumental in providing young Indians with a seat at the global table.

1. The G20 Youth Summits: The G20 Youth Summits (Y20) provide a space for young leaders from across the globe to engage in discussions on pressing global issues, such as economic stability, climate change, digital transformation and social justice. These summits bring together young professionals, students and youth-led organizations to share their ideas with policymakers. Indian youth delegates at these summits have represented the country's interests and contributed to shaping the global agenda, with a focus on sustainable development and inclusive growth.

2. Youth as Stakeholders in Multilateralism: The G20 has recognized that youth are crucial stakeholders in addressing global challenges. Through its focus on multilateralism and global cooperation, the G20 has given Indian youth the opportunity to engage in multilateral diplomacy. Indian youth leaders have increasingly participated in working groups, such as those on climate action and digital economy, allowing them to advocate for policies that will shape the future of their generation.

3. India's G20 Presidency: India's presidency of the G20 in 2023 marked a milestone for youth engagement in foreign policy. During its presidency, India emphasized youth empowerment and inclusive global growth, creating a platform for young voices to be heard. Various programs and events were organized to ensure that youth perspectives were integrated into G20 discussions, reinforcing India's commitment to fostering global youth leadership.

Challenges and Opportunities Ahead

While the involvement of India's youth in foreign policy is growing, several challenges remain. For one, the foreign policy establishment is still dominated by traditional actors and creating more opportunities for youth participation requires breaking down institutional barriers. Moreover, many young people, especially those from rural areas or marginalized communities, may still lack access to platforms that enable them to engage in foreign policy discussions.

However, the opportunities for youth engagement in foreign policy are also expanding. The rise of digital diplomacy, increased access to global forums and India's active role in multilateral institutions such as the G20, the United Nations and the BRICS have created new pathways for young people to influence global decisions.

India's youth is increasingly shaping the nation's foreign policy landscape, reflecting the broader shifts in global diplomacy and governance. Over the past decade, the involvement of young Indians in foreign policy has transformed from passive observation to active participation. Platforms like the G20 have played a crucial role in this transformation, empowering youth to contribute to global discussions on issues that will shape their future. As India continues to rise on the global stage, its young leaders will be key to ensuring that the country's foreign policy remains inclusive, innovative, and forward-looking.

In the coming years, it is essential for the government, academic institutions, and civil society organizations to continue fostering an environment where young people can engage in diplomacy and international relations. The future of India's foreign policy will be shaped not only by seasoned diplomats but also by the emerging generation of youth who are eager to play their part in building a more interconnected and prosperous world.

Rising Geopolitical Stature in Changing Global Order

India, often described as an "Incredible Country", is emerging as a formidable player on the global stage. With its rich cultural heritage, demographic strength and strategic location, India is increasingly being recognized for its growing geopolitical influence. As global power dynamics shift, India's role in the changing world order has become more pronounced, positioning it as a key-actor in both regional and international affairs. This chapter delves into India's ascent in global geopolitics, examining the key drivers behind its rise and its evolving role in the global order.

India's Geopolitical Evolution: From Non-Alignment to Global Engagement

India's geopolitical journey has been shaped by its historical approach to international relations, characterized by its policy of non-alignment during the Cold War. Under the leadership of Prime Minister Jawaharlal Nehru, India sought to maintain its sovereignty and strategic autonomy by not aligning with either the Western or Eastern blocs. The Non-Aligned Movement (NAM) became a cornerstone of India's foreign policy, emphasizing peaceful coexistence, anti-colonialism and mutual respect for national sovereignty.

However, the post-Cold War era ushered in a new phase of global geopolitics, where India began to recalibrate its foreign policy to engage more actively with global powers. The economic liberalization of the 1990s marked a turning point, as India opened its economy to the world and began pursuing deeper diplomatic, economic and security ties with major countries. This shift laid the foundation for India's current geopolitical stature, where it now balances strategic partnerships with the United States, Russia and China while advocating for a multipolar world order.

India's Strategic Strengths in Geopolitics

Several key factors underpin India's rise as a global geopolitical power:

1. Demographic Dividend: India's population, which surpassed China's in 2023 to become the world's largest, is one of its greatest strengths. With a youthful population and a rapidly growing middle class, India has the potential to shape global economic trends. Its vast human capital provides an enormous workforce, fuelling its economic growth and technological innovation.

2. Economic Growth: India's robust economic growth has played a crucial role in elevating its global stature. As one of the world's fastest-growing major economies, India is projected to become the third-largest economy by 2030. This economic prowess has increased India's influence in global trade negotiations, multilateral financial institutions and international markets.

3. Military Capabilities: India's growing defence capabilities, including its status as a nuclear power, have positioned it as a key player in global security discussions. With one of the largest and most technologically advanced armed forces in the world, India plays a pivotal role in maintaining stability in the Indo-Pacific region. Its defence partnerships, particularly with the United States, France and Israel, have further enhanced its strategic capabilities.

4. Geostrategic Location: India's location at the crossroads of South Asia, Central Asia and the Indian Ocean gives it significant strategic importance. The Indian Ocean, a key maritime route for global trade, is of particular interest to India which seeks to protect its maritime interests and secure critical sea lanes. India's position also makes it a vital player in regional security issues from the stability of Afghanistan to the management of China's growing influence in the Indo-Pacific.

5. Soft Power and Cultural Diplomacy: India's cultural and historical ties with other nations, combined with its soft power appeal, have helped build diplomatic goodwill. Indian cinema, yoga, Ayurveda and its rich spiritual traditions have garnered global admiration. The vast Indian diaspora, spread across the world, has also played a key role in strengthening India's soft power influence. India's leadership in multilateral forums like the United Nations and initiatives such as the International Solar Alliance further demonstrate its commitment to global governance and sustainable development.

India's Role in the Indo-Pacific: Countering China's Influence

One of the most significant geopolitical developments of recent years has been the rise of the Indo-Pacific as a strategic concept. India's role in the Indo-Pacific region is critical, particularly as it navigates the challenges posed by China's growing influence.

1. The QUAD: India's involvement in the Quadrilateral Security Dialogue (Quad), alongside the United States, Japan and Australia, reflects its strategic shift towards countering China's assertiveness in the Indo-Pacific. The Quad aims to promote a "free and open Indo-Pacific," ensuring that the region remains stable, secure and governed by international law. Through its participation in the Quad, India has strengthened its partnerships with like-minded democracies and increased its influence in shaping regional security dynamics.

2. Act East Policy: India's Act East Policy, aimed at deepening its engagement with Southeast Asian and East Asian countries, is another key aspect of its Indo-Pacific strategy. This policy emphasizes economic, political and security cooperation with ASEAN countries and seeks to enhance connectivity and trade links between India and the broader Asia-Pacific region. India's growing ties with countries such as Japan, Vietnam and Indonesia are part of its efforts to balance China's regional dominance.

3. Maritime Security and the Indian Ocean: As a dominant power in the Indian Ocean, India has focused on enhancing its naval capabilities to protect its interests in the region. The Indian Navy has expanded its reach through joint exercises, port visits and maritime patrols, while also building partnerships with countries such as the United States, France and Japan to ensure a stable maritime environment. India's leadership in the Indian Ocean Rim Association (IORA) further underscores its commitment to regional cooperation and maritime security.

India's Role in Global Governance

As global power dynamics shift towards a more multipolar world, India has taken on a greater role in global governance institutions. India's rising geopolitical stature is evident in its leadership in multilateral forums and its advocacy for reforms in global governance structures.

1. G20 Leadership: India's active participation in the G20 has allowed it to shape discussions on global economic governance. The G20 provides India with a platform to engage with the world's major economies on issues such as climate change, sustainable development and global trade. India's presidency of the G20 in 2023 demonstrated its growing influence, as it advocated for inclusive global growth, climate action and equitable access to technology and vaccines.

2. United Nations and the Push for Reform: India has been a strong advocate for reforms in the United Nations, particularly the Security Council, where it seeks a permanent seat to reflect its rising global stature. India's involvement in peacekeeping missions, its contributions to international development and its role as a voice for the Global South underscore its commitment to global peace and security.

3. Climate Leadership: India's leadership in global climate negotiations has further elevated its geopolitical standing. As a major developing country, India plays a crucial role in bridging the gap between developed and developing nations on issues such as climate finance and the energy transition. Its ambitious renewable energy goals, exemplified by its leadership in the International Solar Alliance, have positioned India as a key player in global climate action.

India's Relations with Major Powers: Navigating a Multipolar World

India's approach to foreign policy has been characterized by a delicate balancing act as it navigates relations with major global powers. In an increasingly multipolar world, India has pursued strategic partnerships with the United States, Russia and China, while maintaining its commitment to strategic autonomy.

1. India-US Strategic Partnership: The Indo-US relationship has evolved into a comprehensive strategic partnership, with cooperation spanning defence, trade, technology and regional security. The two countries share common interests in countering China's influence in the Indo-Pacific and promoting democratic values. India's designation as a Major Defence Partner by the United States and the signing of key defence agreements, such as the Logistics Exchange Memorandum of Agreement (LEMOA) has strengthened bilateral ties.

2. India-Russia Relations: Despite growing ties with the United States, India has maintained a close relationship with Russia, particularly in the defence sector. Russia remains a key supplier of military hardware to India and the two countries share a long-standing partnership based on mutual respect and historical ties. India's balancing act between its relationships with the US and Russia reflects its commitment to maintaining strategic autonomy.

3. India-China Relations: India's relationship with China is marked by both cooperation and competition. While the two countries share significant economic ties, border disputes and China's growing influence in South Asia and the Indian Ocean have strained relations. India's focus on strengthening its defence capabilities and forging alliances in the Indo-Pacific is part of its broader strategy to counterbalance China's rise.

Conclusion

India's rise as a global geopolitical power is one of the defining features of the changing global order. As the world moves towards multipolarity, India's strategic importance continues to grow, driven by its economic strength, demographic dividend and geostrategic location. Whether through its leadership in the Indo-Pacific, its role in global governance institutions, or its relationships with major powers, India is playing a critical role in shaping the future of global geopolitics.

As India continues to assert itself on the world stage, its ability to navigate complex global challenges while maintaining its strategic autonomy will be crucial. India's rise is not only a reflection of its growing national power but also a testament to its incredible potential as a global leader in the 21st century.

India's Economic Rise and its Influence in the World

India, the world's most populous democracy, has emerged as a major global economic power. Its transformation from an agrarian economy at independence in 1947 to one of the largest and fastest-growing economies today is a remarkable narrative of resilience, innovation and strategic policymaking. As India accelerates toward becoming a $10 trillion economy, its influence in global affairs is growing multi-fold, shaping the geopolitical, economic and cultural contours of the 21st century.

India's economic growth story can be traced across distinct phases:

1. Post-Independence Foundations (1947–1991):

India adopted a mixed economy model post-independence, emphasizing self-reliance and heavy industrialization. Despite challenges like poverty, food insecurity and low literacy, this period laid the groundwork for a diversified economy.

2. Economic Liberalization (1991 Onwards):

The economic reforms of 1991 marked a watershed moment. Under the leadership of Prime Minister P.V. Narasimha Rao and Finance Minister Dr. Manmohan Singh, India dismantled its License Raj, opened up to foreign investment and embraced globalization. Key impacts included:

- Doubling of GDP growth rates.

- Expansion of IT and services sectors.

- Rise of India as a global outsourcing hub.

3. The Digital and Infrastructure Era (2000–Present):

India's recent economic rise has been driven by:

Digital Revolution: Initiatives like Digital India and Aadhaar have boosted financial inclusion and e-governance.

Infrastructure Development: Investments in roads, railways, ports and airports, including ambitious projects like *Bharatmala* and *Sagarmala*.

Start-up Ecosystem: India is now the third-largest start-up ecosystem globally, with unicorns emerging across sectors.

Green Economy Initiatives: Transitioning to renewable energy, with solar and wind power leading the charge.

India's economic growth has averaged 6–8% annually in the past two decades, solidifying its position as the fifth-largest economy globally (nominal GDP) and the third-largest by purchasing power parity (PPP).

Key Pillars of India's Economic Growth

1. Demographic Dividend:

With over 65% of the population under 35 years, India's young workforce is a significant asset in driving productivity, innovation and entrepreneurship.

2. Technology and Innovation:

India's IT and software services sector contributes over $227 billion annually to the economy. Emerging technologies like AI, blockchain and fintech are further boosting India's technological prowess.

3. Manufacturing Renaissance:

The Make in India initiative aims to make India a global manufacturing hub. Sectors like electronics, automotive and defence manufacturing are expanding rapidly.

4. Agricultural Transformation:

While agriculture employs nearly 42% of the workforce, policies like PM-KISAN, digital agritech start-ups and reforms in agri-marketing aims to modernize this vital sector.

5. Global Trade and Diplomacy:

India's robust trade partnerships, participation in multilateral forums like G20 and strategic free trade agreements (FTAs) are crucial for its economic integration with the world.

India's Influence on the Global Stage

India's economic ascent is reshaping its global role in multiple domains:

1. Geopolitical Influence:

Strategic Partnerships: India's partnerships with countries like the US, EU and Japan focus on trade, defence and technology.

Leadership in Global South: India's initiatives in capacity-building, particularly in Africa and Small Island Developing States (SIDS), enhance its role as a leader of the Global South.

2. Multilateralism and Global Governance:

India plays a prominent role in global institutions:

As a founding member of the International Solar Alliance (ISA), driving global solar energy adoption.

Championing climate action and sustainable development in forums like G20, BRICS and COP summits.

Advocating for UN Security Council reform, positioning itself as a voice for equitable global governance.

3. Cultural Diplomacy:

India's cultural soft power—through yoga, tourism, Bollywood, cuisine and festivals—strengthens its global image. Campaigns like Incredible India and initiatives like the International Day of Yoga have amplified India's cultural reach.

4. Technology and Digital Leadership:

India's success in space technology, marked by ISRO's Chandrayaan-3 and other missions, underscores its scientific prowess. Additionally, its tech-savvy diaspora is shaping global policies in Silicon Valley and beyond.

5. Economic Corridor Development:

India's infrastructure projects, such as the India-Middle East-Europe Economic Corridor (IMEC) announced at G20 2023, aim to reconfigure global trade routes and supply chains.

Challenges in Sustaining Growth

India's economic rise, while impressive, faces several hurdles:

1. Income Inequality: The wealth gap poses risks to inclusive growth.

2. Climate Vulnerabilities: Rising temperatures and erratic monsoons threaten agriculture and infrastructure.

3. Skill Gaps: Rapid automation demands upskilling of the workforce.

4. Geopolitical Tensions: Regional conflicts and dependency on global markets impact economic stability.

Future Trajectory: India at 2047

India's rise as a global economic superpower will hinge on its ability to:

- Leverage green technology and transition to a net-zero carbon economy.

- Foster innovation ecosystems and emerge as a leader in AI and space exploration.

- Deepen global trade ties and lead South-South cooperation.

- Invest in human capital, emphasizing education, health and skill development.

By 2047, India is expected to rank among the top three global economies, playing a pivotal role in shaping the world order. Its rise will not only uplift millions within its borders but also contribute to global prosperity and stability. India's economic story is not just a narrative of growth; it is a testament to the power of democracy, diversity and determination. As it continues its ascent, India is poised to be a cornerstone of the global economy and a beacon of sustainable and inclusive development.

Viksit Bharat Vision and Role of India's Youth

India stands at the cusp of transformation, aspiring to become a developed nation under the vision of *"Viksit Bharat"* (Developed India) by 2047, the centenary of its independence. This ambitious goal transcends economic growth, aiming for inclusivity, sustainability and global leadership. At the heart of this vision lies the immense potential and passion of India's youth, who form the backbone of the nation's progress. With 65% of the population under 35 years of age, India's demographic dividend presents an unparalleled opportunity to accelerate its journey toward development.

The *Viksit Bharat Vision* is more than an economic ambition; it is a comprehensive developmental framework emphasizing:

1. Inclusive Growth: Bridging the urban-rural divide, uplifting marginalized communities and ensuring equitable access to opportunities.

2. Sustainability: Achieving growth while preserving natural resources and combating climate change.

3. Technological Advancement: Building a digitally empowered society and becoming a global leader in innovation and technology.

4. Global Leadership: Enhancing India's soft power, participating actively in global governance and addressing transnational challenges.

5. Quality of Life: Providing universal access to healthcare, education, housing and a dignified standard of living.

The realization of this vision demands collective efforts where India's youth play a pivotal role as innovators, change-makers and leaders.

India's Youth: The Catalyst for Change

Youth are not just beneficiaries of development but active contributors to it. Their energy, creativity and resilience are essential to achieving the *Viksit Bharat Vision*. The contributions of India's youth can be mapped across key domains:

1. Leadership in Nation-Building: India's youth are increasingly taking leadership roles in governance, policy-making and social entrepreneurship. Initiatives like the National Youth Parliament and programs such as the PM YUVA Mentorship Scheme are empowering young voices in decision-making.

2. Driving Technological Innovation: Start-ups like BYJU'S, Ola and Zerodha, spearheaded by young entrepreneurs, are revolutionizing education, mobility and finance. India's youth are key players in fields like AI, biotechnology and renewable energy, contributing to the nation's global technological footprint.

3. Advocates of Climate Action: Young Indians are at the forefront of combating climate change, participating in initiatives such as Fridays for Future India and leading local conservation efforts. Their commitment to sustainability aligns with India's goals under the Paris Agreement and SDG 13 (Climate Action).

4. Promoting Social Inclusion: Youth-led NGOs and initiatives are addressing social issues such as gender equality, education for all and poverty alleviation. Programs like 'Teach for India'

and '*Kanyashree Prakalpa*' demonstrate how youth can drive inclusive social change.

5. Strengthening India's Cultural and Global Identity: Indian youth contribute significantly to cultural diplomacy, showcasing the richness of Indian traditions on global platforms. Through cultural exchanges, participation in international forums like the G20 Youth Summit and leveraging social media, they project India's soft power.

Key Challenges Hindering Youth Contribution

Despite their potential, Indian youth face several challenges that need addressing to unlock their full capabilities:

Unemployment: Skill gaps and lack of opportunities hinder youth from contributing effectively to the economy.

Education Quality: Access to quality education and bridging the urban-rural education divide remain pressing issues.

Mental Health Awareness: Increasing stress and lack of mental health support impact productivity and creativity.

Gender Disparities: Gender-based barriers prevent equal participation of young women in development.

Policies and Programs Empowering Youth

The government has launched several initiatives to empower the youth and integrate them into the nation-building process:

1. Skill India Mission: Equipping youth with employable skills.

2. Start-up India: Encouraging entrepreneurship with financial and regulatory support.

3. Digital India: Enhancing digital literacy and creating opportunities in the tech-driven economy.

4. Khelo India: Promoting sports and fostering talent for international competitions.

5. National Education Policy (NEP) 2020: Transforming education to be more inclusive, equitable and skill-oriented.

Youth's Role in Shaping the Future

The journey toward a developed India requires active participation from the youth in:

1. Shaping Policies: Engaging in platforms like youth parliaments and influencing governance through advocacy.

2. Building Grassroots Movements: Mobilizing communities for education, health and environmental initiatives.

3. Promoting Digital Transformation: Leveraging digital tools to create scalable solutions in sectors like agriculture, health and education.

4. Fostering Unity: Celebrating diversity and combating divisive forces through dialogue and collaboration.

5. Becoming Global Citizens: Representing India in global forums and contributing to transnational solutions for challenges like climate change, cybersecurity and pandemics.

A Call to Action

The Viksit Bharat Vision is a collective dream that requires the unwavering commitment of every Indian, especially its youth. As torchbearers of change, the youth must embrace their role with a sense of responsibility, creativity and purpose. The government, educational institutions, industries and civil society must work collaboratively to empower young individuals, equipping them to overcome challenges and seize opportunities.

India's youth hold the key to transforming the nation into a developed, sustainable and inclusive powerhouse. Their journey is not just a path to individual success but a shared commitment to a brighter, more prosperous future for all. The dream of Viksit Bharat is within reach—and it is the youth who will lead the way.

India's G20 Legacy

I recall the statement of our G20 Sherpa, Amitabh Kant where he mentioned "The most complex part of the entire G20 was to bring consensus on the geopolitical paras (Russia-Ukraine). This was done over 200 hours of non-stop negotiations, 300 bilateral meetings, 15 drafts".

India's G20 Presidency was not just a diplomatic milestone but a historic achievement that underscored the nation's ability to drive consensus, deliver outcomes, and showcase leadership on the global stage. During its presidency, India successfully facilitated a record number of Outcome Documents, demonstrating its commitment to inclusive, action-oriented multilateralism. These documents serve as tangible evidence of India's proactive role in addressing pressing global challenges while aligning with the ethos of "Vasudhaiva Kutumbakam" – The World is One Family.

The unprecedented number of deliverables and declarations cemented India's position as a bridge between the developed and developing worlds, reflecting its priorities of inclusivity, sustainability, and resilience.

On 27 July, 2023 External Affairs Minister Dr. S. Jaishankar made the statement in Rajya Sabha that India has been able to focus attention on the most pressing challenges faced by humanity, during its G20 Presidency. He said, emphasis was laid on Mission LIFE for empowering climate-friendly lifestyles, popularisation of millet to address the challenge of food security, and the use of technology to transform the lives of people.

India assumed the G20 Presidency at a critical juncture when the world was grappling with challenges ranging from economic recovery post-pandemic to geopolitical tensions, climate change, and inequality. Against this backdrop, India's leadership focused on fostering global cooperation with an emphasis on actionable outcomes rather than mere rhetoric.

Under the overarching theme of "One Earth, One Family, One Future", India positioned itself as a problem-solving nation and consensus builder. Its strategic priorities were built on the pillars of:

- Sustainable Development Goals (SDGs)
- Digital Public Infrastructure (DPI)
- Inclusive and Resilient Growth
- Climate Action and Energy Transitions
- Strengthening Multilateralism

India's presidency ensured that global conversations were inclusive of the Global South while maintaining cooperation among major economies, resulting in a record-breaking number of outcome documents that addressed diverse and significant agendas.

The G20 under India's leadership delivered over 200 outcome documents and more than 112 working group agreements, an unparalleled achievement compared to previous presidencies. These outcome documents covered a wide array of topics and demonstrated India's leadership in achieving consensus in a fragmented global order.

Key aspects of India's record-breaking outcome documents include:

1. Focus on Global South and Emerging Economies

India gave an unprecedented voice to the Global South by incorporating their concerns into outcome documents. The Presidency emphasized:

- Debt relief for vulnerable nations
- Access to climate finance
- Developmental priorities of Small Island Developing States (SIDS) and Least Developed Countries (LDCs)

The inclusion of these issues in the Delhi Declaration and other key deliverables reflected India's commitment to global equity and solidarity.

2. Consensus Amid Geopolitical Divisions

The global environment during India's presidency was marked by deep geopolitical divides, particularly surrounding the Russia-Ukraine conflict. Despite these challenges, India's diplomatic acumen enabled the drafting of inclusive and non-polarizing documents such as the G20 New Delhi Leaders' Declaration. This achievement proved India's ability to mediate and build consensus.

3. Climate and Sustainability Action

India prioritized climate action through:

- A focus on energy transitions and the role of renewable energy
- Agreements on Climate Financing to support developing economies

- Advocacy for the Blue Economy, ocean conservation, and biodiversity preservation

The outcome documents emphasized climate resilience, adaptation strategies, and technology transfer for sustainability, aligning with SDG 13 (Climate Action).

4. Digital Public Infrastructure (DPI)

India's G20 Presidency showcased its success in developing Digital Public Infrastructure as a model for global adoption. Outcome documents emphasized:

- Digital inclusion for equitable growth
- Promoting DPI as a tool for financial inclusion and delivery of public services

India's experience with platforms like UPI and Aadhaar was highlighted as a global best practice, leading to agreements promoting DPI cooperation among G20 nations.

5. Women-led Development

A critical highlight of India's presidency was its emphasis on gender equality and women-led development. Outcome documents included actionable recommendations for:

- Improving women's participation in the workforce
- Addressing gender gaps in education and skill development
- Promoting female entrepreneurship and leadership

This emphasis aligns with the United Nations SDG 5 (Gender Equality).

6. Strengthening Multilateral Institutions

India's presidency reinforced the need to reform multilateral institutions such as the United Nations and World Bank to better address the realities of the 21st century. Outcome documents highlighted:

- The importance of inclusivity in decision-making structures
- Increased representation for emerging economies
- Key Highlights: The New Delhi Leaders' Declaration

The centrepiece of India's G20 Presidency was the adoption of the G20 New Delhi Leaders' Declaration, a consensus document reflecting India's diplomatic finesse. It included commitments on:

- Global economic stability and growth
- Climate financing and renewable energy
- Food security and supply chain resilience
- Advancing SDGs
- Addressing geopolitical tensions through dialogue

The declaration set a precedent for achieving consensus despite global divisions, making it a hallmark of India's presidency.

India's Soft Power Projection

India leveraged its G20 Presidency as an opportunity to showcase its cultural richness, diversity, and values. Initiatives like "Tourism for LiFE (Lifestyle for Environment)" and promoting traditional art, yoga, cuisine, and heritage sites during G20 events reinforced India's soft power. Outcome documents also highlighted India's leadership in sustainable tourism as a key economic driver.

Legacy of India's G20 Presidency

India's record number of outcome documents will have a lasting impact on global governance. By delivering actionable solutions and amplifying the voice of the Global South, India has redefined its role as a global leader and a champion of multilateralism. The outcomes of India's presidency provide a roadmap for sustainable and inclusive development. They address the world's most pressing challenges while inspiring hope for a better future.

Conclusion

India's G20 Presidency was a masterful demonstration of its soft power, with the Leaders' Summit at Bharat Mandapam in New Delhi standing as a testament to its cultural and intellectual heritage. The historic backdrop of Nalanda University, showcased prominently during the dinner hosted by President Droupadi Murmu, symbolized India's ancient legacy as a global center of learning and knowledge exchange.

This was further amplified by the iconic Konark Wheel, which graced the summit venue, representing the timeless continuum of progress and dynamism rooted in India's spiritual and scientific traditions.

Together, these symbols reinforced India's narrative as a civilizational beacon that bridges the past and future, offering the world not just lessons in history but also pathways to shared prosperity and sustainable development. Through these carefully curated elements, India projected its ethos of "Vasudhaiva Kutumbakam" (the world is one family), resonating deeply with the G20 theme and the global community.

India's G20 Presidency was a resounding success that delivered on its promise of being inclusive, action-driven, and transformative. By achieving a record number of outcome documents, India set new benchmarks for global cooperation, demonstrating its ability to lead with vision, diplomacy, and pragmatism. The presidency enhanced India's stature on the global stage and reaffirmed its unwavering commitment to building a more equitable, sustainable, and interconnected world.

India's legacy as a consensus builder and a harbinger of change will inspire future presidencies, leaving behind a blueprint of collaboration, inclusivity, and progress.

G20
भारत 2023 INDIA
4th Tourism Working Gro
& Ministerial Meeting
Goa
19th - 22nd June, 2023
G20
भारत 2023 INDIA
ONE EARTH • ONE FAMILY • ONE FUTURE

References

https://www.g20.in/content/dam/gtwenty/Indias_G20_Presidency-A_Synopsis.pdf

https://www.g20.in/en/

https://www.amitabhkant.co.in/

https://tourism.gov.in/sites/default/files/2023-06/G20%20Tourism%20Outcome%20Document%20and%20CS%2C%2021%20June%202023.pdf

https://carnegieendowment.org/research/2023/11/the-indian-g20-presidency-taking-stock-of-key-outcomes?lang=en

https://economictimes.indiatimes.com/news/india/59-increase-in-tourism-in-jk-after-g20-meet-lieutenant-governor-manoj-sinha/articleshow/102752571.cms?from=mdr

https://www.newsonair.gov.in/india-has-been-able-to-focus-attention-on-most-pressing-challenges-faced-by-humanity-during-its-g20-presidency-eam-dr-s-jaishankar-makes-statement-on-indias-foreign-policy/

https://travtalkindia.com/g20-to-prop-up-tourism-growth-singh/

www.ingramcontent.com/pod-product-compliance
Lightning Source LLC
LaVergne TN
LVHW061550070526
838199LV00077B/6985